AN EMOTIONAL ENEMA...

Let That Sh*T Go!!

Brigette Hall West

DEDICATION

To: Goldie Hopkins
(a.k.a Mildred Iwilda Hopkins David)
March 27, 1913- September 27, 2003

Aunt Goldie: Thank you.

I'm so glad I got to say it to you when you could see it in my eyes.

TABLE OF CONTENTS

Acknowledgements

First I want to acknowledge and thank The Holy Trinity, for without you I would have never uttered the words "You need an emotional enema!" You always have a way of speaking through me things that have never entered my mind beforehand. You never tire of me being a whiny, bratty, spoiled-rotten child of yours. Thank You for carrying me through so many things and elevating me to this point in my life. It is my hope that, with the remaining time I have on this side of Glory, I will be diligent in honoring Your Universal simplistic laws, planting seeds of Your goodness, watering seeds with Your Hope, and reaping Your harvest in its due season. God the Father, God the Son, and God the Holy Spirit... You do it for me. Thank You.

Thank you to my writing coach... You were the first person who didn't know me personally that believed in this project without reading anything more than the title. Those first emails strengthened my resolve and the first conversation iced the cake. Thank you for your undying support. To all of my "along the journey" and pre-publishing readers: Stacie Wyatt, BR Burns aka "Snow", Robert Quintana Hopkins, and Darrell Richardson: thank you for your honesty and feedback. Without your help, this work would not be as polished as it is.

To my sister LaTasha, I will always be there to "rub your back" no matter what! To my couthers (cousins by blood, *brothers* by living arrangements): Detauras, Kelvin, and Terrance Hopkins; we had the best childhood ever. I am proud of each of you... no matter what! To my spirit sisters: Shawna Dupree, Lisa Hamm-Hardeman, Elizabeth Thompson-Beavers, Macquiva Bermudez-Vega, Monica Allen-Graves, Karen Elem Love, Sandra Groesbeck, and Lezley Jon, thank you for always sharing with me. Sharing truly is caring. To Howard Green, MBA, you are the best *single* father I know. To Efrin Vega, the best *married* father I've met; you keep it one hun'ed! Thank you both for being true friends.

To my mentors James Peters, MBA and Gigi Edwards-Bryant, MBA, I love you both. The two of you never think any idea I have is too crazy or any dream is unobtainable. You share in my entrepreneurial insanity and teach me more in ONE thirty minute conversation a year than working with some people every day! When I grow up, I wanna be just like you!

To the West family; thank you for welcoming all of us into your life and family, and accepting us as your own. You have truly taught me the meaning of family.

To all of my Facebook family, all of my Crockett (especially the Dead End), Tyler, Austin (12th & Chicon), and Milwaukee families (especially Urban Day and Walgreens-Fox Point), all of your love and support is unmatched. To my Texas College, Sam Houston State University, and University of Phoenix-Milwaukee families, each of you gave me memories that will last a lifetime. Thank you.

To all the descendants of Katy Hopkins (1830-19??) and the Jones and Wilbourn descendants; you are the smartest, strongest, sassiest, and sexiest family walking the face of THIS earth and I'm proud to share your DNA.

Finally, to my husband, my heart, my rescuer, Larry West, Jr. and our children Tamiyra, Larry, Lisa, Michael, and Lawryn: words can never express the joy each of you give me individually and collectively. Because of you, I now believe in "love at first sight!" God blessed me with the likes of you to be His little ambassadors of His omnipresence. I wish all families could experience the unconditional, heroic love you have given me. You all know I'm a few cards shy of a full deck, yet you love me anyway. You are the best husband and children one could ever have… today.

Where it always begins….

•

Let That Sh*t Go!   West

INTRODUCTION

Introduction

Why are you so bitter? No really, **why** are you so bitter? Why **are** you so bitter? Why are **you** so bitter? Why are you **so** bitter? Why are you so **bitter**?

And…why are you so bitter, again?

Did your husband, wife, boyfriend, girlfriend trample all over your heart? Did they play "yo-yo" with your feelings only to leave you? Did they leave you *after* you helped them get to the top of their game? Did your husband, wife, or significant other cheat on you… repeatedly? Did they lie to you about cheating? Did you walk into your home, only to find your spouse or significant other having sex… with someone other than you? And when asked why did they cheat… they blamed you?

Did you ever fall in love with someone that refused to or was incapable of loving you in return? Did you give, incessantly, your time, your ears, your advice, your heart, and your money to this person? In the words of songwriter Diane Warren "…*Have you finally found the one you've given your heart to, only to find that one won't give their heart to you? Have you ever closed your eyes and dreamed that they were there, and all you can do is wait for that day when they will care?*" And after all of that giving, all of that work, planting, nurturing… all you have to show for it is bruised emotions and a broken heart?

Did you wake up one morning to find out *you* were the "other" woman/man… that the person you had been in a relationship with was actually married and had no plans of leaving their spouse? Have you, after being hurt by a past lover, decide to swear off having a committed relationship? Yet, every morning you awake, do you secretly long to wake up beside someone that is meaningful you? Have you had the opportunity to seriously date someone that you thought was fantastic but, because they had one child too many, you made your decision not to get too deeply involved? At the time you stated reasons of not wanting to be responsible for someone else's child, or not wanting to have to deal with "drama". But now that their children are grown and successful, and you see how fulfilled their lives have become you are interested in rekindling a love unrequited. Do you feel you are getting mixed messages from that person? Could it be they are no longer interested in you beyond being friends? Do you feel you missed out on something special?

Did your father use you as a paycheck by allowing a Green Card seeking illegal to marry you when you were only 16? Did your father, mother, or other caregiver physically and emotionally abuse you? And because you were abused as a child, did you decide you would reason with your child and allow them to "find their own paths" and not give boundaries to your child? Were you a victim of domestic violence? Did you vow that you would never let anyone close to you again for fear of being abused again? Were you molested by your uncle or aunt as a youth? Did you keep that guilt and shame hidden from your parents for fear of being blamed for what someone else did to you?

Did you dedicate 20 years of your life to a company only to get "canned," was given an engraved pencil and pen set, because you no longer fit into the organizational structure? Did people continuously second guess your abilities when you were trying to create and establish something that would be of significant benefit to you AND them? Did you retire only to lose your pension because some greedy bastard "made off" [pun intended] with your money?

Did the person you repeatedly helped in their time of need not reciprocate the favor during your time of need? Then during tax season, did they brag about how much money they made for the year while you sat in front of them counting pennies to get $1.00 together for a six-pack of noodles at Dollar Tree? Did these same people help someone "on the outside" of your circle instead of helping you... a close friend or family member?

Were you once at the top of your chosen career? Did you have the entire world screaming your name? Did everyone want to be you-the rainmaker? But you, being human, made one wrong step... one side step, ONE... and the same people that used to want to be you have now turned on you and are calling for your head on a platter for being... less than perfect? After making them millions of dollars from allowing them to use your name, your image, your gifts and talents, did you get dropped from the well-oiled moneymaking machine?

And then, and then, and then.... after giving her a better way of living, taking her from being a nanny to a queen, "creating" her and her image, upgrading her from coach to First Class, giving her your last name and your credit cards, taking her from a credit score of 250 to 795, and giving her platinum preferred entrance to any event she wanted to attend, a kid or two... and even if it was your fault... did your wife take a golf club to you?

And how long ago was that?

....
....
....
....
....
....
....
....

....
....
....
....
....
....
....
....
....
....
....
....
....
....
....
....
....
....
....
....
....
....
....
....
....
....
....
....
....
....
....
....
....I thought so.

If these things happened more than a year ago **and** you are still holding on to what "they" did, provoked or unprovoked... at fault or not at fault... you are definitely *emotionally constipated.*

Consider this: It takes food approximately 24-hours to course through our systems, feeding our bodies and eliminating the waste. According to various digestive researchers, waste elimination begins 30 minutes **after** food enters your stomach. Thirty minutes! From there, it takes about one to four days for the food to be completely eliminated from our bodies in the form of waste "...depending on how much fiber your waste contains." According to the Mayo Clinic, waste elimination should occur at least three times a week. If you have fewer than three, and the waste is dry and hard, you are constipated.

Now consider this: if you were to eat three meals a day, for 30 days, and retained **all** the waste from **all** those meals in your body for a month, you would undoubtedly be in some serious physical pain if not dead from the toxic build up. Thus, retaining waste in your physical body for longer than a month, say a year, would definitely be a deadly situation. So this begs the question; why do we hang on so dearly to... *emotional waste?* Why?

This brief overview and basic understanding of the physical digestive system is what led to thoughts about how and what we cling closely to emotionally and mentally. Further thoughts lead me to what I'd like to call the *emotional digestive system.* Just like our physical body has an intake valve and output system, so do our thoughts. Our thoughts and feelings are akin to the food we eat, in that thoughts feed our minds like food feeds our bodies. Words and thoughts are to the *emotional* digestive system as food is to the *physical* digestive system. Many psychologists and psychiatrists agree that there is a correlation to positive or negative thinking and its effect on the physical body and contributing factors to various diseases.

The book of Proverbs explains to us "…For as he thinketh in his heart (mind), so is he." James Allen (1864-1912), an early 19th century writer, put it this way in his book *As a Man Thinketh*:

> Man is made or unmade by himself. In the armory of thought he forges the weapons by which he destroys himself. He also fashions the tools with which he builds for himself heavenly mansions of joy and strength and peace. By the right choice and true application of thought, man ascends to the divine perfection. By the abuse and wrong application of thought he descends below the level of the beast. Between these two extremes are all the grades of character, and man is their maker and master.

> …As a being of power, intelligence, and love, and the lord of his own thoughts, man holds the key to every situation,(*underlining added my me*), and contains within himself that transforming and regenerative agency by which he may make himself what he wills.

Thoughts, therefore, can strengthen you and build you up like a mighty castle. Conversely, thoughts can tear you down by creating problematic areas in your life and, as a result, you will begin to suffer from… well… thought constipation or rather *emotional* constipation… because you are carrying around an excess of *emotional waste*.

The word *emotional*, whose root word *emotion*, is defined as "…*pertaining to or involving feelings;* [anything] *determined by **feeling*** *rather than* **reason** (dictionary.com)." According to Random House Dictionary, the word *emotion* is derived from the French word *esmotion*, which was derived from the Latin word *ēmovēre* which means "to move... to set in motion".

As defined by Merriam-Webster (1997), w*aste*, then, is "*garbage, rubbish, excrement, sewage.*" Additionally, *waste* is defined as "*...gradual loss or decrease by use, wear, or decay... damaged, defective, or superfluous material...*" and additionally "*...being wild and uninhabited, desolate, empty, unproductive, ruined, devastated, discarded as worthless, defective, or of no use...*"
By combining these two definitions to create and define 'emotional waste' we have:

> To set in motion [a state of being] involving feelings, determined by feelings and not reason [that is] garbage, excrement, and sewage [which causes] gradual loss or decrease [of] use, [that is] damaged, defective, desolate, empty, ruined, and unproductive.

I know, right? I had to re-read it myself and I wrote it!

If you are serious about moving forward with your life and want a straightforward approach to doing that, keep reading. If you are looking for a method to "unblock" your emotions, this book is for you. I will warn you, however. This book is not written for the faint at heart. I share with you my life; the good, the bad, and the ugly. If you have an aversion to certain four letter or other unsavory words, this book is not for you.

If you are morally pure, this book is not for you. Although I have never as much as *held* a joint in my hands, let alone put one or had one put to my lips, I am guilty of other frowned upon acts of which I share in these pages. I make no apologies or excuses for my experiences. It is these experiences that have made me who I am and had I not had them, this book would not be possible.

I write with the thought of how a biological enema and laxative work… whether you take it orally or rectally, it can and does cause discomfort and sometimes some tears- depending on how backed up you are. Nevertheless, once you have gotten all that … shit… out of your system, you feel better, livelier, and are essentially healthier (…not to mention a few pounds lighter). Therefore, this is my attempt to help you find much needed relief of all the toxic torment and frustrations to which you have been exposed.

The form of this book is autobiographical with added research on covered topics of discussion. Therefore, to the best of my recollection, the personal events and experiences I share with you in these pages are real. And they are mine. They are my memories. They are my experiences. They are my perceptions. They are *my* reality. Additionally, because it is my life on paper, it includes scriptural references… with a twist. It was impossible for me to write and not make references to *my* ultimate self-help book. If scripture is a problem for you, this book is not for you.

The stories shared here are not intended to hurt anyone but to demonstrate that by making thoughtful choices, you can rise above the situations and circumstances that come with being alive, living long, and being human. It is my personal belief that others understand and respond better to real situations as opposed to hypothetical ones. I do my best to be as candid as possible.

The stories and struggles I share that are not personally mine, I have changed the names and sometimes the gender reference to protect their identity. So, even if the situation sounds familiar, as my daughter says, "Ma! You have over a thousand friends on Facebook!" I personally know ninety-five percent of them. Other stories I share I have found via researching various internet sources and written texts. Some instances were so common; I combined events to add to the sensationalism and to show how ridiculous it is to hold onto things long since passed.

This is an accumulation of stories wrapped in a self-help concept. You will be asked to do some reflecting.

You will be asked to talk to yourself... out loud.

You will be asked to write out your thoughts.

You will be asked to get up and move; to take action.

You will be instructed on how to develop an action plan.

By combining my personal experience with research from some of today's top thought leaders, it is my hope that you will find your... release... by effectively using *An Emotional Enema*. This is my journey, one that I am still on. This is some of my pain and, fortunately, some of my healing... all of which began in my childhood. Additionally, many of the things I write about are very prevalent in American communities today and, likewise, relevant to today's globalizing community. So, again, I ask you:

Why... are... *you*... so... ***bitter***?

In the words of a former statistics professor, at Sam Houston State University, Dr. Kercher: "Think! Then speak!" Yes, take a long moment and think about all those who have done you wrong. Think of all those people that have let you down... repeatedly... disappointing you time... and... time... and time again. Think of all those who have disrespected you; those who have taken your kindness as a weakness; those who have mistreated you, abused you, and left you. You know the ones of which I speak; those who, as soon as you hear a certain song, their face appears in the forefront of your mind. Stop pretending. You know exactly who and what I'm talking about.

If there is no one around you but the Spirit and this book, say the following out aloud....

"(persons' name) _____ you did me wrong! And I deserve better!"

Now say it like you mean it!

Now say it with passion!

Now say it with conviction!

Feel better? Keep reading.

As with any form of medication, self-help, recovery program, or any other type of healing process, this book does not offer guarantees. This is my journey. This is simply a compilation of much personal reflection, much introspection, various processes, and much healing that I've received and I wanted to share it with you in hopes it will help you obtain emotional health.

I made it... and am still making it... and so can you.

Chapter 1:

INGESTION

Avoid fruits and nuts. You are what you eat.

~ Jim Davis

We've all heard the saying "You are what you eat!" This old adage tries to encourage us to eat good, nutritious, healthy foods and to develop and maintain balanced eating habits. It also cautions us about the pitfalls of over indulging in junk foods that have less health promoting benefits. There is another part to this saying, however, that is less frequently used and is often left out of the quotation: "From your head down to your feet." Although I believe this is referring to the totality of the nutrition provided by quality foods to the physical body, I also see it having holistic meanings as well.

Every organic thing has a means of ingesting. Human, animal, and plant all ingest our respective "foods" into our digestive systems and we are thereby given what is needed to have sustainable healthy systems. Yet, unlike the others, we humans ingest thought. My Dr. Dolittle-like son, and many others, would argue that animals have thoughts as well, but... that's another book and a gift I don't have. But for human beings, thought ingestion is something often talked about in an esoteric manner. We are frequently challenged to "Think positively!"... "Think about pure things!"... "Think happy thoughts!" But how, exactly, is this done when so much of what we see tells us there is nothing positive, pure or happy? The above quote gives us a clue.

Just as our physical digestive system has a means of intake, so do our thoughts. Our mouths are the intake valve to our digestive system. Our brains are the intake system to our thoughts. In order to have a healthy physical body, you have to be mindful of what you physically eat - of what you ingest. This is because what we put into our physical bodies is exactly what we get out of our physical body. Likewise, our brains require the same mindful feeding from our thoughts.

Daily, we are bombarded with negative information. Our brains are constantly placed in a state of negative emotional overload. If the radio isn't playing negative broken-hearted music, the radio talk shows and talk show hosts are talking about some tragic event. The television news channels also seem to report only death and destruction. The internet is full of negative "freedom of speech" writings. The movies and premium cable channels are forever promoting the sale of sex, the use of drugs for recreation, and even death for the highest thrill. While all of these have a market... the money made from these mediums proves this to be true... if nothing else is entering into your brain and, consequently your mind, nothing else can come out.

Let me explain it to you this way: If you walk into your kitchen, open the cabinet, take out a glass, turn on the tap, fill it with water, and sit the glass on the counter, what is in the glass?.. **WATER**! And what can you pour out of the glass? **WATER**! Believe it or not, thought ingestion is just that simple. You can only pour *out* what you pour *in*. Period.

Another way of thinking about it is in terms of agriculture. If a farmer planets a row of sweet potatoes, a row of mustard greens, and a row of tomatoes, he will not and cannot get from those rows a tree of peaches, a coop of chickens, and vine of grapes. He will only get out of the ground, sweet potatoes, mustard greens, tomatoes, which is *exactly* what he put in. So undeniably, what you constantly put into your mind, what you continuously expose to your brain and mind, is the only thing that can and will come out of you.

In some psychological and medical circles it is believed that some people are predisposed to being negative. I am inclined to agree with this group. It is my personal belief that this can be traced back to gestation, the time before birth.

At the moment of conception, you began to change. You went from one cell, to two cells, to four cells, to eight cells, to sixteen cells and so on until you became a full blown human fetus. All of the nutrition you received came from your mother. As your organs began developing, your brain too began to process information. If your then environment was filled with negativity you, undoubtedly, may exhibit more negativity and view life more negatively than others.

Since you are a combination of two people, genetics certainly play a tremendous role in making you who you are. Environment also plays an equally vital role in you becoming the person you are. Consequently, I believe that during development, after initial conception, learning also begins the moment brain formation starts.

According to John J. Ratey, M.D. our brains continually change throughout our lifetime. In his book *A User's Guide to the Brain: Perception, Attention, and the Four Theaters of the Brain* he explains it this way:

> The brain is not a computer that simply executes genetically predetermined programs. Nor is it a passive gray cabbage, victim to the environmental influences that bear upon it. Genes and environment interact to continually change the brain, from the time we are conceived until the moment we die. And we, the owners- to the extent that our genes allow it- can actively shape the way our brains develop throughout the course of our lives. (Ratey, 2003, pg. 17)

The above indicates that even when you were in your mother's womb, your brain was subject to both the genetics that formed you *and* the environment you were living in. In essence, you were experiencing, to a certain degree, the same things your mother did because you were living inside her. *She* was your environment.

According to resent research, it has been identified that babies are able to hear while inside their mother's womb. During one study, headphones are placed on the expecting mother's womb and various genres of music (hip-hop, to classical, to country western, etc.) are played and then, through the awesomeness of ultrasound technology, the fetus is observed. Interestingly, the unborn children reflect a preference. Those exposed prior to the test to country western display a preference to such. Those exposed previously to hip-hop, likewise, display a preference to such.

Thus, as an in utero child you could hear conversations, even if muffled, experience laughter, joy, misery, stress, overexertion, and a host of other emotions, including anxiety. If you, as a growing and developing human are experiencing these things, it is my belief that this could be a starting point for your emotional constipation. That being said, with my own children, I can remember the various states of mind and environments I was in during their gestation. Allow me to introduce them to you.

TAMIYRA: Cool as a cucumber

At age 18, a recent high school graduate, and pregnant with my first child, I was very laid back, nonchalant, not worried or stressed about what I was going to do in life with a new child or how I was going to do it. Although I was very calm, at times I could be downright outspoken and belligerent. There was much controversy surrounding me throughout the duration of this pregnancy. For starters, I was a church girl. My parent was the church secretary and I was the president of the youth choir and drill team.

Additionally, I was (and still is) a member of a very affluent family in my community. My family was one of those families whose last name could get them out of a botched bank robbery, even though we're caught red handed with ten money bags, while others would be sent straight to jail without passing go or collecting $200!

My family has always been one of the pillars of the community and my grandparents and great-aunt had either been or presently were teachers in the school district. And if that weren't enough, I was pregnant by someone much, much, much, much, *much* older than me. Nevertheless, being who I was at that time, I took it all in stride and things rarely bothered me.

During this gestation period, I was very pensive, careful and intentional about everything I did. Nothing ever surprised me. Even my pregnancy was no surprise. The night I got pregnant I informed her father, in a very matter-of-fact manner that I was ovulating and we should wait until another day to be intimate. He, having never fathered a child at almost forty, repeated the same thing he had told me a few times before; he was "…sterile." I, somehow, knew better than that and kept telling him in a matter-of-fact way, "I'm going to get pregnant."

I wasn't really concerned about having his child because 1) I really liked her father and 2) I thought we would make are really cute and smart baby. It was that simple with me. I had no intentions or grandiose delusions of him marrying me or anything of that nature. He was a good conversationalist, had a great sense of humor, and he enjoyed and appreciated the fact that I was highly intelligent as well. I simply liked him and believed that having his child wasn't the worst thing in life… even though he thought he was sterile. Subsequently, I was really at peace with myself, my decision, and my situation. Our daughter, interestingly enough, is quite the same.

She has a very cool exterior. She hardly ever fretted as an infant or a child. She, too, is very intentional about things she does. She is very straightforward and direct. As a 3 year old, after attending daycare for one day she decided to drop out because, as she told me... "I don't know these people."

And today, as a young adult, although she wanted to drop out of college, she has stayed the course in-spite of being around "...these children." She didn't get side-tracked and, at the time of writing this chapter, has one semester left to complete and receive her Bachelor's degree from the prestigious Howard University.

Additionally, she is not easily provoked or aggravated about things she has encountered. When faced with being homeless one month after her relative reneged on their offer to allow her to live free of charge and made to feel very unwelcome in their home, she simply called me and told me what was happening without raising her voice or any stress. *Once* she cried! Only *once* because she did not understand why a **blood** relative would, after being *offered* financial compensation and *refusing* to accept BECAUSE they were the only family each other had in the DMV (DC, Maryland, and Virginia) area, would a month later begin to treat her in such an unwelcoming manner.

Her heart was broken because this was... her family. They shared the same DNA. Nevertheless, after the initial shock, she moved on and moved out quickly.

She has rarely been interested in following the crowd... doing what everyone else is doing. Once she tried to sneak and drink, but got caught; once she wore something inappropriate to school and, again, got caught... so she stopped trying to sneak and remained true to her intentional self. She is how I was. She is very calm, very frank, and very intentional... much like I was as I carried her.

To illustrate just how calm I was, I share this about the day she was born:

I went into labor in the early morning hours. I calmly told my Aunt Goldie I thought it was time because I had seen the *bloody show*. She sent my cousin across the tracks to rouse my grandparents to come stay at our house with my younger siblings. I woke my sister up and she and I did our customary ceremonial happy song... "We're going to the _____ (fill in the place)" as we got dressed. I don't know who was more excited, me or my sister. I made one phone call to my child's father and left a message.

After my grandparents arrived, Aunt Goldie, Mama Jimmie, my sister and I hopped into *the boat*- a 1982 sky blue Lincoln Continental. As Aunt Goldie leaves the then Commerce Street and enters Loop 304, she turns on the emergency lights. I look at my sister. My sister looks at me. And we simultaneously burst into the most explosive joyous laughter... although mine was cut short from a contraction.

There I was riding in the backseat of the car **laughing** as my Aunt Goldie sped around Loop 304 in Crockett, TX, at two in the morning... with the hazard lights on! Now, Crockett, TX, in 1989 had approximately 8000 citizens, one fully functioning traffic light, a Dairy Queen, a Sonic, a "chicken shack" called Ames, two grocery stores, a Wal-Mart that wasn't a supercenter... and... there really was absolutely **no** need for those hazard lights!!

My grandmother was in a panic and started fussing because she thought my sister was laughing because I was in pain...which made my sister, then 14, laugh even harder, making me laugh harder... in-between contractions. Most mothers I shared this story with said they were too terrified to even notice the nuances my sister and I recognized. I was free from worry. I was free from stress. I was free from fear. I was as cool as a cucumber, as is Tamiyra.

LISA: The artist and temperamental

While carrying Lisa, my life and situation were completely different. I had moved away from home to Tyler, TX with my child and enrolled in Texas College. Since I had Tamiyra, my Aunt Goldie got me an apartment and I would get a ride to school. Somewhere along the lines of my upbringing, everyone failed to tell me that an apartment came with a monthly fee called rent. I had never heard the term "rent" in association with housing. I thought you just paid for the space much like you go to the store and buy goods! Therefore, I thought my apartment was "paid" for.

I remember the day I saw the pink slip on my door. I called my parent and proceeded to tell her that the note said I owed over $500 and I didn't understand for what. She said, "Brigette. That's your rent." I said, "Rent? What is that?" She proceeded to try to explain what it was and I rebutted, "But I thought you paid for that already!" Long story short, she paid for me to get out to the lease and I moved in with my youngest aunt. This would start a myriad of difficulties.

During Lisa's gestation I honestly didn't want to be pregnant. That's not to say that I didn't want my child... I just didn't want to be pregnant! There's a difference. I already had one child and myself to feed, school to attend, assignments to complete; how was I going to provide for another child if I were pregnant?

Accordingly, I refused to believe that I was pregnant until I started showing in late June, early July. I preferred to think something happened and I was experiencing early, very early onset menopause! You've heard the statement, "Mind over matter"… well my mind was completely over the matter of my being pregnant. Perception is reality… until reality changes your perception.

It was the hottest summer ever and there I was pregnant. At age 20, I recall being very irritable, fretful, easily frustrated and discouraged. Unlike my first pregnancy, I experienced emotional highs and lows and often resorted to eating and sleeping to "settle my nerves." My food of choice was the *family-sized* fried okra from Church's Chicken ®. It *had* to be the family size or I simply could not eat it… No matter how hard I tried or how hungry I was, I *had* to have the family-sized fried okra!... and a pork chop.

During this gestation, my emotional state was truthfully shot! Some days I was happy. Some days I was most miserable. Lisa is quite the same. She can be the most loving child some days and the most irritably, irritated… and irritating… child the very next.

Notably, during the summer of Lisa's gestation, her father and I were poor college students. School was out so the dorms were closed. A few times we slept in his Chevy Citation, us in the front seats, Tamiyra in the back.

Even though I had four aunts living in the same city, none of them were comfortable with having me, my child, and my live-in boyfriend living with them. As long as it was just me and my child, I was welcomed to stay. But adding him presented the element of "shacking" and they would not be guilty of condoning such sinful behavior…even if that meant their pregnant niece and her two year old daughter had to sleep in the car.

So, there were many nights we would sleep in the car if he couldn't find himself somewhere to crash for the night. Many of those nights we slept right outside one of my aunts place, unbeknownst to them. Thinking about those nights reminds me of how un-fearful, resilient, and resolved one can be when faced with difficult choices.

Even though he had an okay paying job we couldn't afford the going rent rates. After a while one of my aunts allowed us to live in my great-grandmothers' dilapidating wood-frame house. While the house was comforting and familiar to me, it had leaking pipes, which meant the water had to be turn on and off from the outside. Furthermore part of the house was rotting and the floor was caving in. Indeed, this was not the best place for a two year-old and a pregnant woman to be living.

There were many days I would just lie in the bed and cry. I needed income to get enough money to help pay for an apartment, but couldn't find employment that fit my needs or his work schedule. I thought about becoming a stripper to make money. Thought about it but I couldn't do it. I even thought about being a prostitute. I didn't know what to do. I didn't know where to turn. Thankfully when August came and students started returning to the area, we were able to move in with a mutual friend, Anthony "Tony" McQueen, who needed a roommate, but not before my heart was brutally crushed.

On one particular day before moving in with our friend, one of my aunts informed me that she contacted my biological mother and one of my uncles. She told me that she hated to tell me what had been said but felt strongly that I needed to know the truth. She proceeded to tell me that she had explained to them my situation and the present lack of employment opportunities and how this contributed to making a tough situation worse. She told me she tried her best to convince them that there was more to the situation than she felt comfortable sharing but, felt they should help because I was family, after all, and needed a hand up.

Despite her pleas for assistance, they both, nevertheless, told her to "let her [me] hit it!" You can only imagine how frustrated and angry and downright despondent I felt. I couldn't believe that two people who shared the same blood as me, and one who had given birth to me, could be so callused, so mean, so uncompassionate.

It wasn't like *I* called them to ask for their help in the first place. I wasn't a drug addict! I wasn't an alcoholic! I wasn't a jail bird! I wasn't thief! I didn't even know my aunt was going to do that! How does a woman deny help to her own child? How does an uncle deny help to his own niece? I cried so hard and so much until finally my aunt told me that crying wasn't going to help the situation and to suck it up because something was bound to come through. She reminded me of what the Word said in Psalms 27:10…

When my father and my mother forsake me, then the Lord will take me up.

I began to think on this scripture. It was as if the Word knew that this day would happen because it did not say "**if**…" it said "**when.**" So, I settled down and began to pray.

A few hours after she told me this painful news, another aunt would come driving around the corner, hooking her car horn, yelling out the window…. "Gigette! Let's go get something to eat!" And just like that, as if a fairy had sprinkled pixie dust over the entire world, my attitude and emotional state changed. Honestly, it was as if the previous events never happened. We went to Shony's and I ate so much and so good!! We laughed and talked and had a good time!

Looking back, I am thankful for THAT day. It was a defining moment for me and my unborn child. Amusingly, Lisa can be so lively and vivacious one moment and in a mood the very next! The moment she was born, Lisa didn't cry or fret. She had both eyes wide open and she literally looked around the room, looked… as in turned her head left then right, as if to say… where is this?

The nurse, my aunt Iwilda, and I all looked at each other aware of how unusual that was. I tried to get the nurse to put her back but she felt like that wouldn't work. When Lisa did decide to cry she was hungry. She drank the entire four ounce bottle of formula. During her grade school years, I would introduce her to her teachers in the following manner: "Hi! This is Lisa. She's an artist and she's temperamental!"

At age 4, after a Head Start field trip to McDonald's, Lisa announced to me that she was going to be a "cooker" when she grew up; at 7 she began cooking on a gas burning stove; at 19 she entered culinary arts school. She is a foodie, it calms her whether she's cooking it or eating it.

Before we go any further, I'm no clinical psychologist but no, Lisa is not bi-polar. She doesn't experience manic modes or extreme depressive states. She is creative and sensitive. Presently she continues to be a full-time student, works two full-time jobs, and is pursuing her dream of being a model. She and I bump heads when she's in her uncensored mode. Indeed, she's just like the candy commercial… "Sometimes [she] feels like a nut. Sometimes [she] don't!" Lisa is how I was.

MICHAEL aka Dr. Dolittle-like: (*He's the baby and I really don't have a subtitle to describe him because he's just my baby!*)

And then there's Michael. His father was the first to be served notice of this gestation. He had been deathly ill for about 3 days and was the one that informed me I was pregnant. On his knees, holding his stomach, and writhing in pain he looks up at me and says… "You're pregnant and it's a boy."

Having no symptoms after a few weeks, I decided to take a pregnancy test. When I looked at the pregnancy test and saw the dark blue plus sign... I immediately thought: "NO! NOT NOW! NOT AGAIN! My baby is in kindergarten! I don't want to start all over AGAIN!!! Lord, please do not give me another girl. I do not want to comb another head. If I have a girl, I will put her up for adoption because combing four heads is just too much." Some priorities I had, huh?

In the month of January, at 25, I was placed on bed rest. During this time, I also moved back home to Crockett and did absolutely nothing the entire pregnancy but eat, have witty conversations with my Aunt Goldie and grandmother (who would pass away just months before his birth), and sleep.

If I didn't like you, you knew it. There was no pretending on that end. Although I loved my cousin-my child-my brother Terrance pre-gestation, he absolutely vexed my soul during the duration of this pregnancy. I would become nauseated at the sight of him. I remember seeing him twenty feet away and literally had to close the bathroom door to keep from hurling!

Additionally during this time, I was very unwilling to share. I was so incredibly stingy. I would hide food in my room and was very reluctant and unenthusiastic about sharing with anyone. Oh and I loved sweets! Never in my life, that I can remember, had I eaten so many sweets. And no, I did not have gestational diabetes.

Another interesting quirk I manifested during this pregnancy is the fact that music had to be playing in my ears for me to go to sleep. Without listening to music, I could not find rest. I remember buying a portable CD player that didn't skip when you walked. Yet, as crazy as it may sound, Michael's behaviors are ridiculously the same. He hates to share his sweet treats… and he rests best with music playing in his ears. And no, after he was born, he was not put to sleep with music playing in the background. It's the darnedest thing.

Michael is bright, charming, witty and intelligent. He is sensitive to the needs of the elderly, hurting people and animals. There isn't an elderly woman that has ever met him who doesn't immediately fall in love with him.

Michael loves conversation, good food, and sweets. He enjoys, to my chagrin, attempting to be the class clown. But as bright and wonderful as he is, Michael is L.A.Z.Y. He has to be coerced into doing his chores, homework, working out, etc. If he likes you, you are his best friend forever, his brother, his cousin, his family. But if he doesn't like you, he really cannot tolerate looking at you! I laugh as I write this because he *is* precisely how I **was**.

I shared these specific points in my past to get you to you to consider what your mental predisposition was coming forth from your mother's womb. Are you still skeptical? How many siblings can you count that have the same parents, the same genetic makeup, but they are so fabulously different? Those of you that have the same mother and father, the same DNA, and were raised in the same house with those same two people that made you… yet you are so and completely different, know exactly what I'm talking about.

It is these observations that lead me to my conclusion that the difference lies in the events and circumstances your mother experienced as she carried each of you. Undoubtedly each of you were "carried" in a different way, with different experiences. Because *her* experiences where different, this helped shape the way *you* received **and** processed information from the beginning when compared to your siblings.

If you are fortunate enough to have your mother still alive, ask her about the circumstances surrounding your birth. Ask her what her life was like during the time you shared her body. Ask her what *she* was like when you shared her body. I am willing to bet, you will discover some very interesting similarities.

If you have a child, or children, think back to your state of being as you carried them (or, fathers, how she behaved carrying your child) and how they emulate patterns formed during their gestation.

Another interesting bit of supportive information is the studies that document identical twins separated at birth. Dr. Ratey explains that differences have been noted in respect to whether the twin child was carried as "...a "front child" or a "back child," a "spleen child" or a "liver child,"..." If any two people would ever be exactly alike, it would be identical twins since they have identical genes. Yet, the way they were carried, their position in the womb, makes a difference to their individualization.

With these thoughts in mind I offer this: the way you *began* ingesting information has some bearing on the way you have continued receiving, processing, and exchanging information since you were born, throughout childhood, adolescence, and on into adult life. Remember, "you are what you eat; from your head down to your feet."

If what you ingested while you were in the womb was restlessness, fear, and frustration, what will and possible has come out of you is restlessness, fear and frustration. Whatever was planted in you from day one is going to come out. I posit, therefore, that emotional constipation can begin in the womb. Whatever the environment you were pre-exposed to undoubtedly affects some of your behaviors.

Emotional constipation can also begin outside the womb. Quite frankly, emotional constipation begins when and where there is too much input and not enough output. For me, it began the year before I entered kindergarten.

CHAPTER 2:

Digestion and Constipation

They know that the tongue is part of the digestive system, which they view as a whole and it is part of Indian philosophy that the tongue helps to eliminate toxins from the body.

~Theodore Welt

*S*tarting school can be a pleasant experience for some children, yet for many others they struggle. Unlike today, when I was a child, many children did not attend pre-school or daycare. Back in the 60's and 70's going to kindergarten was the first experience for many of being separated from their parents or other known family members and of being placed into a room full of strangers- both big and small.

Many kindergarten students experience separation anxiety during the first few days of school until they become acquainted with their classmates and teachers. Kindergarten, therefore, can be a very traumatic time for many children. This was especially traumatic for me. The year was 1976. I was five years old and entering kindergarten.

The previous year my young mother had taken my newborn sister and me back to Crockett, TX for what was meant to be a temporary stay with our grandparents. Her plan had been to return to California, better her situation, and then come back for us. When it came time for my mother to leave, she told me that she was going to the store and would bring me something back; she often used this bribe to keep me from acting a fool. She left for the "store" and I waited and waited and waited and waited... and waited some more, but my mother never came back from the store.

During that span of a year, my 3 month old sister became very ill with thrush. With 4 young girls at home- ages 16, 14 [twins], and 12- and a very small amount of space and resources, my grandparents were at their max. Although both my grandparents where teachers, my grandmother had taken ill some years earlier. That left my grandparents with only one full-time income and eight mouths to feed. So, the decision was made for my sister and me to live with our great aunt, Aunt Goldie and our great-great aunt, Aunt Lula.

My Aunt Goldie, who never had children, had recently built and moved into her new home. She had more than enough space and resources to provide for my sister and me. The only other person that lived with her was her aunt, Aunt Lula. Like Aunt Goldie, Aunt Lula had no children of her own but had taken in and raised her deceased sister's five children. This, interestingly enough, would be my Aunt Goldie's same destiny with the difference being Aunt Goldie would raise her living brother's five grandchildren.

I vaguely remember my aunts, my mother's sisters, spending those first summer nights with me at Aunt Goldie's new house. But I vividly remember crying and running after my grandparents' car once it was time for them to leave. I would literally fall out on the street and cry for minutes on end (we lived at the end of a dead end street… so I was safe.) Even though they lived across the tracks and I could literally see their house from the end of my street, at age four, "across the track" seemed so far, far away. And you must remember my mother still had not returned from "the store."

Also during that year, I would attend an in-home daycare and a preschool. Mrs. Brenette Davis, aka "Teacher" was a pioneer in our community. She owned one of the first in-home daycares in Crockett. She was also a member of St. Luke Baptist Church, the church my family attended. So, as a favor to my grandmother, I went to her house to "be around children my age" (having teenagers for your aunts *and* your friends when you are four years old creates a very *grown* child with a slick mouth). Because she catered to pre-school aged children, my sister did not attend her daycare. I do not remember being at Teacher's daycare for very long but I do recall while I was there I felt very alone and I cried… a lot.

After being in her daycare for a brief period of time, I was accepted into *The Lift Center*. *The Lift Center*, at the time, was a phenomenal government funded daycare program for children ranging in age from infant to age 5. Indeed, it was a Head Start type program. During this time, *The Lift Center* provided diapers, wipes, food, and bedding for the students, unlike today's programs. There was a small library and a cafeteria for the older students to congregate and eat. What brought me the most joy while I attended *The Lift Center* was the fact that I knew my little sister was a few doors away and I could go see her... when I needed to.

I recall going to see my little sister in her room one day. A lady by the name of Mary Black, who also attended our church, was holding my sister and rocking her. My sister was sick again. While I do not recall verbatim what Mrs. Black said to me, I do know that she told me I needed to be a big girl and stay in my own class so I could learn.

Mrs. Black not only recognized that I was having difficulty adjusting, she was also pushing me towards learning how to let go of the things I had no control over and helping me to move forward. I would have been very content being in the nursery room with my sister. But Mrs. Black wasn't having that too many times.

As I write this now, tears fill my eyes because that was a great deal of adjusting for a four year old to experience. I was constantly being shifted from one place to another. I was steadily meeting new people and experiencing new environments before I had the opportunity to fully adjust. I was like a plant being put in one location and soil only to be uprooted and taken to another location and soil before I could receive strength and nourishment from the previous location.

But the wisdom and grace of The Most High strategically placed people in my life, like Mrs. Black, to teach me how to let go. I cannot say I was just being a big sister that was protective or a little girl trying to hold on to the something that would not leave her. But I do know I was eventually able to stay in my own classroom until it was time to go home for the day. Truly, I was being taught early in life how to let go and trust Him.

Constipation

So from May or June of 1975 to September 1976, my emotional intake consisted of: moving from a big California city to a small, country Texas town; my mother going to the "store" and not returning, leaving me with my grandparents and aunts. By July, my sister becomes ill and we moved in with Aunt Goldie. In August/September, I went to Teacher's daycare and then from Teacher's, possibly around November or December, I would go to *The Lift Center* until August 1976. This is a lot to try to try to digest and I had little to no outlet or understanding of all the changes that took place.

I held on tightly to my sister and was most miserable when presented with a change, any change. Holding all this *inside*, with no one present to guide me through or talk to me about all the changes taking place in my new world, my new home, my new space, I became withdrawn and very uncertain when introduced to new things. I became fearful. I had become emotionally constipated.

As I entered the hall of the kindergarten wing in the fall of 1976, I was constantly being reassured by Aunt Goldie that she would return. At this point I was still deathly afraid that she never would. I recall the peach pleated dress that I wore the first day of school. Although I had several clothes, I chose my "Easter dress." I think I liked the way the skirt would fan out when I turned around in it... and it always made me feel pretty. Nevertheless and even with that dress on, at the tender age of five, I had severe abandonment issues.

I remember clinging to her leg and begging Aunt Gold not to leave me. She would try to comfort me by saying, "Brigette, now you know I have to go to work, but I will be back." I remember that conversation would go on and on until she would offer up some bargaining tool... which most times didn't work. I just wanted to be with her.

Why did she have to leave me with people I didn't know? What if they make fun of the way I talk? Are you sure you are coming back? Do you promise? I don't know anyone here. "But Brigette, you know Mrs. Hunter. She lives down the street from Mama Jimmie." And although I didn't have a rebuttal for that, it didn't work initially and I would cry... every day... for months.

My kindergarten class consisted of mostly teacher's children. It was taught by Mrs. Hunter who just so happened to be another one of my grandmother's friends (did I mention that Crockett was a small town) and, as previously mentioned, lived on the same street as my grandparents. I had been to her house on a few occasions since my aunts were about the same age as her children. However, being the teacher, she was not able to attend to me one-on-one. I remember her trying to greet other parents and attend to me. And then Mrs. Maggie showed up. Thank God, for Mrs. Maggie.

Mrs. Maggie Kent, the teacher assistant, immediately saw to taking me by my hand and keeping me close to her side. Everywhere she went, I went. She kept me beside her all day every day. I vividly recall being at recess and laying my head in her lap because I was unable to venture away from her side. Fear of being left again plagued me. My mother had still not returned from the store. She would lovingly ask me, "Brigette, don't you want to play with the other little girls?" To which I would shake my head. "Donkey's shake their heads, young lady. Use your words," she would say. "No ma'am." I would reply.

I'm not sure how long I didn't participate in recess activities, I do remember that I often tried and I just never seemed to quite fit in. Since I had lived in California for the past few years or so I still pronounced the entire word. I spoke "proper." My mother had already done an outstanding job of teaching me the alphabet, my colors, and numbers, how to spell my name, the days of the week, and the months of the year, so "why do I have to learn stuff I already know?"

Furthermore, when my Aunt Goldie sent me to school, I was always impeccably dressed in the latest kid fashions from Dillard's, Lord and Taylor, Niemen Marcus, or Bloomingdale's department stores with a fresh pair of shoes from Stride Rite or Bakers. Each day I went to school, I looked like I was going to church on Easter Sunday morning. As my Aunt Goldie would say, I was "sharper than a rat's turd!" She was old school and believed that whenever you left the house you needed to look your very best.

I shared all of this information about my beginnings to illustrate to you were my own emotional constipation began. Even now, I remember that feeling of abandonment and fear. On the days when she came late because she had a faculty meeting and didn't let me know that she would be late, I often feared she would never return. My mother had not come back from the store. And if I am completely self-disclosing, I would be remised not to mention that even as I wrote the above memories I had to stop and wipe away tears.

I remember feeling so completely alone at school. I felt so abandoned and isolated. I felt lost and hopeless. I felt fearful and ashamed. To put it in the terms of a five year old, I felt very scared.

And yet, I felt so fully relieved and safe when I would see my Aunt Goldie pulling up to get me in her 1965 light blue Ford. Experiencing such emotional highs and lows at ages four and five makes one pause and think of the potential future consequences and repercussions I would face. I marvel at how I made it through. But, as the old adage goes, "what doesn't kill you makes you stronger." However, I was very young going through so many emotional changes while receiving no truthful explanation.

So what does this have to do with digestion? Research tells us that children between the ages of three and ten have rapidly developing brains. Since brains process information, this is a critical period of growth and development.

At the age of four, children begin to develop a consciousness of self... that is they become aware of "self." With the formation of a conscious self, children begin to better understand the world in terms of individualization and can better recognize differences between themselves and others. It is here that children become self-aware and may even begin to become self-conscious... if they experience negative feedback about the noticed differences between themselves and another person or persons. At this age, children begin to rapidly "digest" information, talking large bits of information and breaking it into smaller understandable pieces that fit their world.

Clark and Clark (1939) discovered in their research study that at age 4 children begin to develop self-identification and self-perception. Children at this age are able to consistently differentiate between who they are as an individual and who someone else is. By showing students flash cards of boys, girls, an animal, or object and asking the participants to pick the one that "...looked like them," the majority of the children stated,

"I'm not there." This indicated to the Clarks that these young children had a strong sense of self and who they were.

Now suppose, for a moment, that during this time of constructing a self-identification and self-awareness your world has no stability, no solid ground. The person who is responsible for helping your still developing self-perception become strong, healthy, and secure… disappears. You are moved around in different circles and are expected to make new friends. But that is difficult because you talk with an accent and you also articulate so well that you might as well be speaking a foreign language. You also wear expensive clothing and are overly concerned about messing them up than enjoying recess.

Furthermore, you had never really been around children before. Having aunts that were eight to twelve years older than you as playmates you, functioned on their level and not on the level of… babies. Indeed, you too would face many challenges with your developing self and self-perception. At ages four and five, your developing self-esteem would be under attack.

According to Orth, Trzeniewski, and Robins (2010) the development of self-esteem is strongly impacted by interpersonal relationships. Information presented by North Carolina State University suggests that when children feel valued and accepted by adults and peers that are important to them, healthy self-esteem develops. Since self-worth is multi-faceted, develops through phases and is shaped by experiences, early childhood is a critical time for parents to lay the groundwork for healthy self-esteem.

But what if your parent went to the store and never came back. And what if no adult around you took the time to explain that she hadn't actually gone to the store, leaving you to believe that she just disappeared? What about her self-esteem?

Throughout this critical developmental stage, it is imperative that a child's emotional digestive system- their thoughts, subsequent behaviors, etc. - are protected and cared for. During this period of development, children learn how to trust through interaction with parents and caregivers. When going through life's transitions with children, it is important to assure them that life is full of ups and downs.

It is important to be truthful with children and not build up false hopes in them. This is how children learn to trust their parents and others. Without having a solid foundation of trust on which to build, a young child will have difficulty trusting others and themselves, often developing apprehensions and fears instead of confidence and security.

This period for me was riddled with lies, false hopes, uncertainty, constant changes, instability, and therefore led to fear, separation anxiety, a restless spirit, and a mindset that everyone always leave. It would take a lot of patience from my Aunt Goldie and much independent reading of self-help books to begin to undo the emotional damage I sustained during this one year. Even today it is a constant struggle for me to develop relationships and not revert back to the withdrawn little kindergarten girl in the peach pleated dress.

Before I close this chapter, I just want to clarify something. My mother was not and is not a drug addict, an alcoholic, or anything like that. She was just a young woman, trying to improve her situation through the best means she knew how.

She did finally return from the "store," albeit two and a half years later, ready to pack us up and take us back to LA. She had gotten established and could now properly take care of us. She did come back. But this... this moving my sister and me back to California, did not sit well with several people, namely my grandfather.

It is my understanding that he told her since we were settled in and his sister, Aunt Goldie, had gotten attached to us, he didn't think it would be a good idea to take us back to California. I don't know all of the details. I don't know who said what to whom. I don't remember exactly when she left. What I do know is we, my sister and I, didn't grow up in LA and it would be years before we would see our mother again. When she left this time, she just left.

As we got older, my sister and I would have very few conversations about who, what, when, where, why, and how about our situation. My sister told me once that she felt unwanted... even though she had no memory of ever living with our mother. I shared with my sister that I really didn't fault our mother about leaving us. My issue was more fundamental.

The problem I had with our mother was never getting a card, letter, or phone call on a *regular* basis. She would and did send things but there was no consistency about it. It wasn't like we needed her to call every day, but at least every birthday and holiday. Was that asking too much?

It was her not attending graduations or helping with prom preparations. It was wondering how a mother could just go through life, knowing where your child is but not contact them *regularly*. But, I encouraged my sister, we had to release all of those "idol thoughts" and focus on the wonderful life and opportunities we did have. We were well taken care of and provided for from the time we moved on the Dead End until the day Aunt Goldie passed.

Now before you start passing around judgments, I can honestly say my mother has the highest respect for her father. Even though it cost her relationship with her children, she obeyed and honored her father's wishes. My mother has her own emotional constipation from how everything turned out and not having the typical relationship mothers and daughters have. She too paid a high price and she too had to learn to let go.

She was heartbroken to not be allowed to have her own children back. I know she longed to raise us. I'm sure she wept bitter tears. During conversations when this subject would come up, I have often told her that even though it was not what *she* ideally wanted for us, it was The Master's plan. I've reminded her that had we been raised in LA, we could have been hit by a stray bullet, strung out on drugs, prostitutes, gang members or any other number of urban horrors that befall young females. What is done is done and can't be undone. All we can do now is move forward and do better.

Your story may be similar to this or not. Your story may be worse than this. You may have been raised by your grandparents because one or both of your parents were in jail. You mother may have been or still may be a drug addict and your daddy might be a pimp or a hustler.

You may be a member of a family to which you have no biological connection to, but because your grandmother went to church with a kindhearted woman, you and your sister are now members of a family that loves you more than those that you share DNA with. You cannot undo your mother's decision. What's done is done. Let that shit go.

You may have been raised by both parents yet you've often felt just as alone and abandoned as my sister and me. Your parents may not have been supportive, emotionally, financially, or otherwise. Your parents may have irresponsibly placed you in adult situations during your childhood causing you to have to fend for yourself at an early age.

Your parents may have been so consumed with arguing with each other and having their own way, they were unable to focus on you, your siblings and your emotional needs. I understand. However at some point, you must seek relief from your own emotional constipation. You, too, must let that shit go.

Unfortunately, all of us that were born of a woman came here with our own different needs and were born with our own agendas. Yet none of us, none of us were born with instruction manuals. Every parent is simply making it up as they go along... even after reading parenting books and tips; they still had to modify those suggestions to fit your individual needs. The truth is some parents are simply better at making stuff up than other parents.

I encourage you, therefore, to do the only thing you can do: understand, let it go, and do better. If you don't make a conscious effort to unblock your emotions and you continually to hold on to, packing more and more in, one way or another, an outlet will be made. And incontinence sets in... and release will happen, just when you least expect it.

CHAPTER 3:

CONTROL & CONSTIPATION

Persecutors fear loss of control. Rescuers fear loss of purpose. Rescuers need Victims-someone to protect or fix-to bolster their self-esteem.

~David Emerald

*I*magine you are standing in front of a door. You pull the handle or twist the knob but nothing happens. The door doesn't open. You try it again and again. Still, the door doesn't open. You begin to knock on the door. Still, nothing happens. You try the doorknob or handle again, shaking it with a little more force than preciously. Nothing. You stand there… looking at the door. You decided a different approach might just do the trick. So, you back up and with a sudden burst of energy, you charge at the door leading with your shoulder only to be knocked flat on your ass. You lie on the ground, hurting, and tired from trying to open that door. As you are picking yourself up, someone walks up to you, looks down in your direction and asks, "Are you ok?" You say, "I'm fine, but that stupid door is stuck and won't open." They help you up and say, "Well, why didn't you try the other door?" And, with their free hand, they open the door right next to the one you had been single-mindedly focused on and desperately trying to open. *How would that make you feel? Foolish? Like an idiot? Embarrassed as hell?*

Pulling on Looked Doors (control) in Career Development

The above scenario is representative of so many people and speaks to the concern of trying to control things that are not meant to be. Some of us have a tendency to become so focused on trying to **make** something budge when it just isn't happening. That locked door is representative of many things in life including but not limited to a career path, a relationship, or a business opportunity.

Sometimes in life, we become so obsessed with becoming **_one_** specific thing that we lose sight on other meaningful and fulfilling opportunities. Additionally, we sometimes tend to think there is only **_one_** avenue to achieving our goals of wealth or living comfortably. You may be trying to become a singer, a rapper, a journalist, or a professional ball player but the doors to these paths are locked and are simply not opening.

You have tried to climb over the barrier; you try to place your foot against the wall to get more leverage but still nothing. You tend to put so much energy and focus on this one path instead of trying the next door and moving the hell on. So, there you stand, scratching your head pulling and pushing on... a *locked* door.

While you stand there, you're thinking you've encountered natural opposition and that you simple need to overcome these barriers placed in your path of success. Unfortunately, this is not the case. Many times we naively believe that a locked door is a barrier. We misunderstand and misapply that old mantra "if at first you don't succeed, try and try again." We also misapply our faith by putting *"our substance of things hoped for and evidence of things not seen"* into goals and activities that are not and do not lead to fulfilling our purpose.

Sometimes, more often than not, we continually put valuable energy and effort into something that is honestly and simply not... to... be. You are simply wasting time, energy, and money trying to *make* something happen this is not going to happen because it's not supposed to happen! And as a result, you injury yourself and sometimes others trying to **make** that 'door' open! Many of you reading this book have been guilty of this very behavior. Let me share the store of someone I knew.

There was this young girl I had the pleasure of meeting once. She was tall and thin, relatively attractive... an exotic beauty. People always told her that she could and should be a model. When she got of age, she moved out west with her boyfriend to try to make that modeling career happen.

She found an agent, who booked her a photo shoot, helped her pick photos for her comp (composite) cards, and had those made. She went on "go sees" as well as participated in fashion show after fashion show always coming up just shy of being chosen for a contract. The last fashion show she entered was for an opportunity to go to New York Fashion Week, which would take place two weeks later.

During the show, she would nail her walk on the runway, her poses, her makeup, and her hair styles for casual wear, formal wear, and swimwear. She was edged out by a fellow agency girl by only half... point 5... ½... of a point during the sporty section of the show. Therefore, it would be her fellow agency buddy winning first place and heading to NYC. But that's not the kicker!

The kicker is her follow agency buddy **did not go to New York**! Not only did she not go, but their agent had been unsuccessful in contacting her by phone **and** mail. It was as if the young lady had disappeared and vanished into thin air. Mail was returned with no forwarding address. All phone numbers had been disconnected.

It was at that moment, sitting in my agents' office in Scottsdale, Arizona, at the age of 22, I knew that I was not to be a model, super or otherwise. I had been constantly pulling at a locked door for four years. I had wasted countless energy, time, and money on something that simple was not meant to be in my foreseeable future. And although it was not my destiny to be a supermodel like Tyra Banks or Beverly Peele, it didn't mean I couldn't look like a supermodel! Ha! Just wait until you see me on *The View*!

Before I go any further, let me clarify these thoughts. By suggesting that you move on, I'm not suggesting that you should immediately quit when you attempt something and are met with opposition. I'm not suggesting that you give up on or abandon a realistic dream or set of goals. What I am speaking of is recognizing **when** to move on. In life, some things really are not meant to be. Learning to 1) identify when to move on and 2) actually *moving on* are important to having success in life.

It was not meant for me to be a supermodel or I would have been one. It was not meant for President Obama to become a professional basketball player or he would have been one. It was not meant for Donald Trump to have great hair or he would have it. No, none of these things were meant to be.

At some point, you have to recognize when to stop tugging on that locked door and when to move on to the next one. As my homeboy Kenny Rogers sang: "You've got to know when to hold 'em; know when to fold 'em; know when to walk away; know when to run." And just think had the President or the Donald become fixated on their 'locked doors,' they would not have the successes they enjoy today.

How do you know when it's time to move on you ask? That can be very tricky. I am reminded of something my parent used to say to me: Brigette, no doesn't always mean no. Sometimes it means not now.

In the supermodel situation, that no was firm. People, whole families, just don't disappear in two weeks… not without foul play. And there was no foul play. President Obama had to accept and recognize that although he was good, he wasn't *that* good. Learning to acknowledge when the Universe is speaking is key! And learning to *accept* what the Universe is telling you will allow you to see the unlocked door right next to you.

For those of you that may be aspiring to become professional singers or rappers, you may need to get the opinion of someone who is not related to you and does not travel in your "buddy circle." Find someone that will tell you the whole truth. Many times, family members don't want to hurt your feelings because they see how badly you want to reach that goal.

However, if you are tone deaf, you will only waste precious time, energy, and money on trying to accomplish something that is not meant for you.

Many Americans want to be rich and famous, but most of you think there are only a few select ways to become that. If everyone was an entertainer, there would be no doctors, lawyers, teachers, grocers, restaurateurs, bankers, pharmacies, pharmacists, or fisherman to go get king crab! However there are hundreds of thousands of ways to become rich and possibly famous.

If your parents or school did not do a good job of exposing you to the immense numbers of career opportunities, visit your local library or look up all the careers in listed in the U.S. Bureau of Labor Statistics. There are many options and many people who have made millions, even billions, by doing something non-conventional. Some of these names may be familiar, others not some much. But I present the lives of four remarkable and contemporary people whom I respect and admire for a brief exposé.

Oprah Winfrey

Yes, I started with Oprah because her story truly has me in awe. Oprah wasn't born rich and she is not an athlete, a recording artist, or a movie star (Angela Bassett is a movie star... hey Angela! but Oprah starred in a few movies. There's a difference.) As we all have read, she faced several obstacles growing up. Having lived in Milwaukee, WI for three winters and having worked at a school there, I am completed blown away by her ability to rise above that environment, and from facing all the other tragic events she experienced throughout her childhood and teenaged years.

It truly is nothing short of amazing. As she progressed in life, there were several closed and locked doors she faced. Yet, she kept it moving until she came to the open one. From there she continued to find her way by moving beyond those closed and locked doors. Today, as she is counted the peer of Bill Gates and Warren Buffet, I'm sure as she sits reflecting, she becomes in awe of her own triumphant 2.7 billion dollar net worth life.

Guy Laliberté

Canadian-born Guy Laliberté is the founder and CEO of Cirque du Soleil. Guy started out walking the streets of Quebec and LA playing the accordion and harmonica, often also walking on stilts and swallowing fire! When that did not always pay the bills, Guy decided to move back to Quebec and take a full-time job at a hydroelectric dam. A funny thing happened though. The company's employees went on strike! Recognizing the opened door, he returned to street performing. In 1984, in celebration of Canada's 450th anniversary and with the help of a government grant, Cirque du Soleil was born. Originally, Cirque du Soleil was presented as a once a year project, but Quebec's government wanted a touring event to perform throughout the provinces. Cirque du Soleil, not sports, not music, propelled Guy into his dreams. Additionally, Guy is a professional poker player and a space tourist claiming a total worth of $2.5 billion. How about that for swallowing fire?

Sheldon Adelson

My recent and first trip to Las Vegas got me to thinking about two things: making money and who *owns* "the strip." Sheldon Adelson, only the eight wealthiest American, is the owner and CEO of the Las Vegas Sands Corporation... which owns and operates The Venetian Resort Hotel Casino and the Sands Expo and Convention Center. Born in Boston to Ukrainian immigrants, Adelson worked as a mortgage broker, investment adviser, and financial consultant. He tried his entrepreneurial hand at selling toiletry kits and a charter tour company. But what propelled him into his current wealth was the 1979 computer trade show COMDEX. These shows would last through the 1980s and much of the 1990s. And in 1988, Adelson and his partners would purchase the Sands Hotel and Casino. Trying his hand in different areas, having doors closed in his faced and locked to deny him access, he continued to follow locked door after locked door, closed door after closed door until he found his path to a present net worth (what he gets to take home) of $24.9 billion.

Ursula Burns

First let me say, (((*waving and blowing kisses in the air*)))..................... **I LOVE YOU SO MUCH URSULA! YOU ARE MY SHERO!!!!! LET'S DO LUNCH!!!!!!! CALL ME!!**

Born to Panamanian immigrants, Ursula was raised in New York in tenement housing and would later move into a New York City housing project by a single parent. While I have never been to NYC, my friends Macquiva and Efrin have painted graphic pictures of deplorable conditions. The images are so bad, I wish I could scrub away the images by taking out my brain and giving it a once over with some steel wool. On a recent PBS interview, Ursula humbly and jokingly described moving from the tenement to the projects as "...moving on up... moving from the *really* bad to the bad."

Earning a Bachelor of Science degree in Mechanical Engineering from Polytechnic Institute of New York University in 1980 and a Master of Science in Mechanical Engineering from Columbia University the following year, Ursula used the open doors of education to truly move on up. She has spent her entire career at Xerox because she was not afraid to either try a new opportunity when it presented itself or to speak up.

She began working at Xerox as an intern in 1980, and a year later became a full-time employee. Ten years later, she would become an executive assistant to Wayland Hicks and then to Paul Allaire in 1991. Ursula would go on to become Vice President of Global Manufacturing in 1999, Senior Vice President in 2000, and President of Xerox Group Operations in 2002. In 2009, she would experience two history making events: she would succeed Anne Mulcahy, making this the first woman-to-woman succession in a Fortune 500 company, and she would be named CEO of Xerox- the first African-American female to lead a Fortune 500 company. Ursula did not get stuck pulling on one locked door, which would have hindered her from earning approximately $22.7 million annually.

These people, real people whom are alive today, should inspire you to think bigger than music and athletics as careers. They should also encourage you to stop continuously pulling on the same locked door.   While Oprah and Guy chose careers in entertainment, they cater to different audiences. Sheldon started out "handling" other people's money to having people "hand" him money. Ursula, dedicated over thirty years of her life to a company she now leads. These four, and countless more, are living proof that there are more careers that earn millions of dollar than just sports and music.

If you are not making any progress... chances are you need to move on to the next door. Moving on is not about giving up, it's about making progress. All of these people continued to move forward, without fear of letting those locked doors go. All of them recognized opened doors of opportunity and did not fixate on trying... to... make... this... stupid... door... open. They've all had to let go of that handle. You should too. Who knows? That next door, the door right next to it, could be the unlocked one.

Pulling on Locked Doors (control) in Relationships

These same behaviors, constantly pulling on a locked door, are found in intimate relationships too. Often they manifest themselves by having the same argument, or by trying to get someone to do something that is not in their nature. It can also be exhibited by holding onto disappointments in the relationship. If you have held onto a disappointment and have become downright un-agreeable, you are guilty of repeatedly trying to open a locked door.

If you didn't get your way or have tried to manipulate your spouse or significant other into doing something *you* are insisting on them doing, you are guilty of repeatedly trying to open a locked door. Or if you have continuously complained about something that keeps happening, like asking why the person refuses to put the toilet tissue on the roll with the paper falling *forward* instead of *backward*, and you have constantly been met with opposition, you are guilty of repeatedly trying to open a locked door.

I used the toilet tissue example purposefully because that situation was a real problem for me in a previous relationship. Honestly it is often an area of contention among many couples. For the life of me, I could not understand why... he... just... couldn't... put... the... paper... on... the... right... damned... way! And although we didn't part ways over the directionality of the paper, it wasn't until after I had my emotional enema that I realized the simple solution to this problem. What is it you ask?

Change it myself. Turn it around. Just take the three seconds to reposition the toilet tissue and go on with life. Why continue to get all flustered about the way the butt wipe fall?. If it was being done intentional or unintentional wasn't the issue. I couldn't control why or how it got *on* the roll... but I could control *my* reaction and following actions to seeing the tissue falling behind the roll. I could control *my* subsequent behavior and simply change what I saw. After all, it was me who had the problem.

I am reminded of two situations where I had to teach my children about negative controlling behavior. The first was with Lisa, then nine, and Michael, then four. These two had an argument over what *she* had chosen to wear to school. Tamiyra had reached her point of trying to reason with Michael and he had demanded to speak to me about the situation. I was sitting on the bus when my phone rang.

Michael, in the sweetest little voice ever, proceeded to tell me that Lisa had chosen to wear her "church dress" to school, and that he didn't want her to mess it up. I can still hear the distress in his voice. He was a highly upset four-year old. After I first reassured him that I knew she was wearing the dress, I explained to him that it was picture day and she had to look pretty for her pictures. "Don't you want your sister to look pretty?" "Yes ma'am." "Thank you for telling me, but it's ok that she wears the dress. Now you have to go ahead and get dressed and have a good day at school. I love you." "Ok."

The second situation involved Tamiyra and Michael. On this day, Michael wanted to wear some red socks instead of blue socks. He refused to get dressed if he couldn't wear those red socks. Again, I'm on the bus, heading to work when my phone rings.

"*Mama!*" Tamiyra says. "*Will you please tell Michael to put on these blue socks? He wants to wear the red ones but he doesn't have on anything red!*" "*Tamiyra, isn't he wearing jeans?*"... "*Yes, ma'am.*"... "*No one will see what color socks he has on. Let him wear the red socks.*

You're wasting time trying to make him do something he doesn't want to do. It's ok if he doesn't have anything else on red. What matters is that you leave on time and get to school on time. Ok?" "Yes, ma'am."... "Ok. Have a good day at school. I love you." "I love you, too."

In the Lisa and Michael scenario, Michael looked at Lisa, knew she was wearing something that was not meant for running and playing at school, and tried to make her wear something different. What he did not know was it was picture day and her attire was completely acceptable for the occasion. He understood part of the situation. How often have we made the same judgment calls as adults not fully knowing the situation? As the saying goes... believe nothing you hear and only half of what you see.

Negative control issues begin early. In the Tamiyra and Michael scenario, Tamiyra was so focused on those red socks that she was missing the task of getting to school on time. Indeed, she was wasting time over socks. How often, as an adult, have you wasted time trying to get someone not to wear red socks when no one was going to see them anyway?

In the book *The 7 Habits of Highly Effective Teens*, Sean Covey paints a picture of two circles: a circle of control and a circle of no control. In the circle of control he lists self, our choices, our behavior, our responses, and our attitudes. In the circle of no control he lists items such as parents, skin color, the past, the weather, tuition costs, rude people and comments, or who wins the NBA finals.

I would like to add a few more things to this list. We have no control over being fired, someone else's decisions, our spouses, our friends, teenage or adult children, how someone else drives, someone else's thoughts, birth defects, mental illnesses and physical diseases. So why do we try to control these things?

Control versus Responsibility… A Word on Parenting

Often times we confuse having control with being responsible. By definition, control means to **restrain**… to prevent from doing. The interesting thing I find about this word is control often requires some physical exertion. To "prevent from doing" requires a physical activity. Police officers prevent being retaliated against by placing restraints (physical activity) on the hands.

Highway developers and repair crews prevent drivers from entering their work areas by placing up cones (physical activity) and blocking off the area. Parents of newborns prevent them from getting into various things by doing some physical activity. So control requires physical activity, while being responsible… to allow things to happen… requires restraint.

Responsible parenting does not happen because you are old. Responsible work habits don't happen because your name is on the hotel. Responsible eating does not happen because you simple read the labels. None of these things makes you responsible. Knowing when to apply the restraints and how tightly to apply them, however, does.

Responsible parenting requires the adult to know when, where, and how to apply restraint themselves. In addition to love, children must have structure, boundaries, and consequences. They also have to be challenged, or encouraged, and pushed to do more. Responsible parenting requires developing the ability to not only give them the tools for success, but teaching them how to use those tools and allowing them opportunities to practice using those tools BEFORE they graduate from high school.

During a conversation with the hubs, he mentioned how individualistic I am and made a comment about my children being the same way. I simply replied, "Well they *are* individuals….." As a single parent, I took the opportunity to observe each child and never… and I do mean never, tried to make one child be or do things like the other child. My reasoning was simple; they were born as an individual person. Period.

Additionally, Aunt Goldie did not raise my siblings and me to be the same. Although she expected us to do our best- "our best" was *relative* to us as individuals. She did not expect Kelvin or Terrance to be the athlete that DT was. DT was a football player…Kelvin was a baseball player… Terrance was a basketball player. She didn't try to make either of them BE LIKE the other…she just let them BE! She did not try to make Tasha the writer that I am & she did not try to make me the reader Tasha is. She just let us BE! She demonstrated tremendous **restraint** and ultimately had each of us submissive and obedient.

Sometimes in marriage (and in parenthood) we forget to just let each other BE! We either get caught up in trying to change the other to fit some fairy tale mold…. or some TV relationship in which the couple does EVERYTHING TOGETHER!!! ….or even misinterpret "And the TWO became ONE FLESH" (which is actually talking about representation and accountability)…. We forget that the person we are with is an individual…. Heck even twins are individuals!

I spent the time on this chapter because too many people have serious "control constipation." At some point, we must come to the understanding that we can only control ourselves and our children… and them to a certain extent. However, controlling an adult? Forget about it. We must learn to accept this truth. Self-control and being responsible is the key to moving forward. If we do not learn this truth, we risk developing incontinence.

CHAPTER 4:

INCONTINENCE & SELF-CONTROL

"Remember not only to say the right thing in the right place, but far more

difficult still, to leave unsaid the wrong thing at the tempting moment."

~ Ben Franklin

As I thought about this title, the one topic that continued to come to mind was how the things we try to control the most, the thing we try to hide the most, still has a tendency to leak out... unintended and at the most inopportune times. I remember the morning after President Obama won the election in 2008. At that time, I was working in a very high volume retail pharmacy store that is typically moving something fierce about thirty minutes after the doors opened. But this day, for my entire shift, it was a dead as I had ever experienced during my time there.

Since then, throughout American society, we have all witnessed what seems to be a rise in racism. The operative phrase is "...seems to be..." The truth is, nonetheless, racism has never died. It was secretively trying to be "controlled and maintained" but in the wake of the First African-American First Family taking the White House, people... certain groups of people... just seemed to suddenly developed what I call OED - oral enuresis disorder- and began pissing out and vomiting up those private and hidden thoughts towards African-Americans with blatant remarks of incongruous communal disregard for these four *American* people.

Presently, as I am writing this chapter, President Obama is preparing to run for his second term and it seems that his opponents are simply focusing on "beating" Obama. It seems that there is nothing more important to this group of presidential hopefuls than just getting President Obama out of office. This gives me a serious ax to grind.

Since I have been unemployed and underemployed for going on three years, I and many others like me would like to hear about job creation. Because I was unsuccessful in obtaining employment immediately after my untimely and pretentious termination from a certain pharmacy chain which I will not shop in on the west coast, combined with the outlandish high cost of living in the Seattle metropolitan area, at the writing of this book, my family has been living in a local Extended Stay hotel for several months... and we are not the only family here.

Imagine you, your spouse, your two teenaged sons and teenaged daughter living in a small non luxurious hotel room that has a shower, a two eye stovetop, a mini refrigerator, and a tiny sink. Imagine having your eight year old child having to play in the parking lot because there is no park within walking distance. Imagine having to schedule sex with your spouse because you share a room with your children who have few places to go. These are real situations. These are real people. These families and many others, like us, are not interested in you just saying you want to beat Obama. We want to hear thoughts and see plans to get us back on our feet!

My husband has a great paying job... on paper! We had some money in savings but went through that trying to maintain after I was unable to readily obtain employment. And then one day while at work, he suffered a knee injury, which would put us in a downward financial spiral. Today as I write this book, we are, in essence, without permanent housing. Yet, all "they" can come up with is beating Obama? Tisk tisk. I need to hear your thoughts on getting me a full-time job.

What does this have to do with incontinence? One of the candidates has been quoted as saying he's not concerned with the poor. Another has been quoted as saying that he doesn't want to make "Black peoples" lives better by giving them someone else's money.

These are their thoughts! These are their thoughts that, at some point previously, they have tried to control in public, yet have undoubtedly said these things in the privacy of their homes, country clubs and undiversified religious gatherings. And just as diarrhea takes skill and timing to control the impending gush (I told you this is not for the faint at heart), so does NOT making ridiculous statements such as these.

I had a very good paying position and was terminated under ridiculous circumstances. Yet after a series of rapidly accumulating unfortunate events, here we are. Homeless. If in your incontinent speech you inform me that I am of no concern to you, why would I vote for you? If in your incontinent speech you tell me that you are not going to make my life better, why would I vote for you? I have a Bachelor of Science degree in Psychology, an MBA, 17 credit hours towards a PhD, and I am a Black person who needs to earn money from someone else to make my own life better. Yet he thinks I'm looking for a hand out.

How can I give you my vote for the incontinence of your views of me? I can't and won't, and neither will many others in my position. Just as actual diarrhea is lose and messy, and often requires the person to take a shower afterwards, so is diarrhea of thought and the mouth. If it is in you, no matter how you try to control it, it will come out at the most inopportune time leaving you looking bewildered, foolish, and lacking skills to recognize those ever telling signs that you should head to the bathroom before you shit on yourself!

Before I close this section, I am reminded of a conversation I was having with a friend and a high school classmate. They proceeded to tell me about their dog that they had recently gotten and... because of his color... they decided to call him "nigger." Yes, you read this correctly. I was stunned to the point of being speechless. And yes, this friend and classmate is White. When I heard them say that, I think I lost my hearing and developed temporary amnesia because I honestly don't remember anything after that.

These are the types of things that are upsetting to me as an African American, yet I am supposed to *not* take offense. Was it meant to be harmful? No. Was it said in malice? No. Nevertheless it's definitely not the most intelligent thing to say to your Black friend.

I've had a white dog, but I didn't call her nor *think* to call her white-she-devil-that-likes-to-buy-black-boys-expensive-sneakers... or saltine... or redneck... or PWT- poor white trash. Her name was Snow. If only people would do as my professor used to say in my statistics class, "Think! Then speak!" the world would be a much better place.
And if, by chance, you are reading this book, you are still my girl and I still love you!

Apologies: Not acceptable

One thing that continually vexes me is how adults expect, need, yearn for an apology when they are hurt... advertently or inadvertently... by someone they have been involved with. But apologies really are for children. An apology is a learning opportunity to teach children to be aware of what they do. An apology also teaches children to think about their actions before they do them. Lastly an apology should only be given when real unintentional acts are committed.

However, if someone, some grown someone, hurts you by some intentional act they did, no apology is owed. Whatever they did... say spending all the bill money on street pharmaceuticals... they meant to do! They thought about it. They knew what should have been done. Yet, they chose to do something differently... with the hopes that you wouldn't find out.

Therefore, when an offending adult gives an apology, they are not apologizing for their **behavior**, they are merely saying words to appease you. They have already done exactly what they wanted to do in the first place. At this point, the person is merely blowing smoke up your ass!

.I learned a long time ago that a mouth will say anything! But a sincere heart… a sincere heart is followed by ACTION. When a person is truly remorseful about something they have done, the offense is not planned and the error is always followed by a change. This is why Jesus said, "If you love me you will keep (do) my commandments." Actions truly speak louder than words. But why do we want words?

Something else that continually baffles me is how grown people expect **another** grown person to respond to their demands as if the other adult were a child. And even children do not blindly do what you say because you asked! We've all experienced that defiant two year old in the grocery store, adamantly saying "NO!" So why do grown people consistently attempt to make another grown person like them, love them, respect them, understand them, appreciate them, desire them, support them and their dreams, and on and on? I believe the problem lies with understanding the differences between an expectation and a guarantee. Let's see what those differences are.

The root word of *expectation* is *expect*. By definition, and for our usage here, expect means to look forward. A synonym for *expect* is *hope*. Merriam-Webster says: "*hope means to await some occurrence or outcome. Hope implies* **little certainty** *but suggests confidence or assurance in the* **possibility** *that what one desires or longs for will happen.*"

Investigating the definition of *guarantee*, we find it to be more contractual as in things will be done because compensation of some form has taken place. I think of a guarantee as an equal exchange for services rendered. By entering a grocery store, we guarantee the store owner that we will pay for any items before we leave. A guarantee is an "if... then..." statement: If I want these apples, then I will pay the price for them before I leave the store.

Unfortunately, people are not "if... then..." statements and an expectation only carries with it "...little certainty..." So when you fully understand the difference in these two words and their proper functions, without any doubt, your relationships will improve because you now realize that just because you *expect* something there is no *guarantee* of it happening. Even in marriage, there are no guarantees because your spouse is human and subjected to failure.

Having had time to read and contemplate the error of your ways, I pose to you a few questions to ponder: Has anyone ever told you that you are controlling or demanding or unreasonable? How long have you stayed in a relationship that wasn't mutually beneficial or satisfying? How long have you sat brooding over a relationship gone badly?

How long have you waited for your spouse or significant other to apologize for hurting your feelings? How long have you blamed a former colleague for taking your idea and for getting promoted as a result? How long have you been upset with that preacher or pastor? How long have you walked around upset because you misunderstood the difference between an *expectation* and a *guarantee*?

But there you are, at that locked door, trying to make this grown person give you an insincere and meaningless apology. Then you believe, to your later disappointment, since they apologized to you they love you. I come to give you a truth: an apology does not equal love. No.

God is love.
And God makes no apologies.

The Look of Love

When my husband and I were dating, I would often ask him, "Why do you love me?" His reply was always the same: "Because I do." After being married for some time, I have asked him this same question periodically and his answer still remains the same... "Because I do."

It took me awhile to truly understand the meaning encased in his simply answers. In other words, there was nothing that I did to cause him to love me, nothing I said, no move I made, no trick I played. He loves me because he chooses to love me. (But let him tell it, I tricked him.)

Many people, Christian people, have often pondered the question, "Why does God love me so much?" There is nothing that we did or can do to evoke the love that is bestowed on us. God loves us simply because He *chooses* to love us. Therefore if we, supposedly created in the image of the Most High, are truly striving to be like <u>Him</u>... why do we insist on making people prove their love to us? And why do we try to *make* someone love us? Either they love you or they don't. Period. And we will know they love us because their *actions* will say... I love you.

My husband, though he is not perfect, he takes care of my needs. He is kind to me. He is gentle with my emotions. He doesn't crowd me. He tells me "no" when the situation calls for it. He laughs at my jokes. He confronts me and calls me to the carpet when necessary. He supports most of my goals and dreams... most because some things I come up with are out there!

There are things he finds less favorable about me, but he doesn't dwell on those. He chooses to look beyond my need to take up ¾ of our king sized bed... even though I'm a buck-0-five soaking wet, with a brick in my back pocket. He and I come from two different parts of the country, were raised by two completely different philosophies and family dynamics, so sometimes communication is an issue. We're both the oldest child and think "I'm" always right. Nevertheless, he continues, daily, to choose to love me and, as a result, I can't help but to love him back.

The best explanation is this:

> Love suffers long and is kind; love does not envy; love does not parade itself,
>
> It is not puffed up; does not behave rudely, does not seek its own (will), is not easily provoked, thinks no evil; does not rejoice in iniquity, but rejoices in the truth; bears all things, believes all things, hopes all things, endures all things. Love never fails. But whether there are prophecies, they will fail; whether there are tongues, they will cease; whether there is knowledge, it will vanish away. (1 Cor. 13: 4-6 NKJV)

Self-Control, Mistakes and Choices

Have you ever heard the saying, or has anyone ever said to you, "The only thing you can control is yourself"? I'm sure you have heard it and may have even read it in some other book. This phrase is something that I have often told my son, Michael, when he would come home after being suspended from school for doing something silly in class. Many times he was simply following the crowd, going along to get along. He has often tried, and failed miserably, to convince me that his behavior was someone else's fault. He would tell me what this person or that person did to make him take the firecracker and throw it down the hallway.

Time and time again I would ask him, "Michael, who controls you? You! No one can make you do anything. Either you are going to want to do whatever it is or you're not. Unless someone has a gun to your head, no one can make you do anything... and even then, Michael, you still have a choice." Michael is a teenaged boy and it is a guarantee he will be given this talk repeatedly.

The sad truth is, while Michael is yet to reach adulthood, many adults are guilty of teenaged behavior. So many adults are annoyingly guilty of blaming someone else for their bad behavior and choices. Some of us tend to go through life following the crowd and blaming our decisions on someone else.

We tell ourselves that we continue to work on a job we don't like *because* we have to feed our families. What's closer to the truth is we have gotten comfortable with the status quo and really don't want to go through the process of looking for and interviewing for another position. We tell ourselves that we can't go back to school *because* we don't have time or money to invest in an academic degree. What's closer to the truth is we are afraid of being the oldest person in the classroom and not being able to retain information like we once could. We tell ourselves that we pay bills *because* we have spouses or significant others to answer to. What's closer to the truth is we need a roof over our heads and hot water to bathe in.

Now I know there are men out there that don't pay bills because their sister, girlfriend, wife, or significant other does it for him, but the truth of the matter is, at some point, barring he is homeless living on the street and in various shelters, he is going to have to provide a roof over his head and hot water for a bath. Even people that live in group homes have to pay for their care. And while all of these situations may provide unique barriers to entrance, the underlying truth is we do or we don't do because we choose to do or we choose not to do.

How many people do you know that are thirty and over and need to hear this same reprimand because they continually make excuses for their poor decisions? I say thirty because while you are in your twenties, you really are still learning and trying to figure things out. But the year before you turn thirty, there should be some serious accountability taking place.

By thirty, there is no "The devil made me do it!" By thirty, there is no "What had happened was…" By thirty, you have been around enough blocks, been on enough dates, been in enough situations to know what the outcome is going to be before you carry out the action. By thirty, you know that if you spend all night Saturday night dancing and partying, you are either going to be late for church, fall asleep in church, or simply not make it to church at all. Whether or not your parents have talked to you frankly about being responsible and not placing blame on someone else for your actions, at some point in adulthood, ownership has to be taken for both your personal choices and professional growth and development.

I have a friend, Skip, who is notorious for blaming everything on someone else. His girlfriend got pregnant; it was her fault although he didn't use a condom. He didn't get promoted; his supervisor was racist although he was never on time for work and would never cover for anyone else. His Honda got repossessed; it was his brother's fault for not paying him a loan back. He can't get a job because he has a record. He can't keep a job because he always has to go to child support court. No matter what the situation is, it's always somebody else's fault for his choices and his irresponsibility.

Now I know that many of you reading this book have often heard someone say that in life you will *make mistakes*. I'm here to tell you that that statement is a lie. An innocent meaning lie, if there is such a thing, but a lie none-the-less. ***There are no*** _**mistakes in life**_. Absolutely zero! Zilch! There are, however, choices... good choices and bad choices. And unfortunately there are no crystal balls to let you know which one is which until after it is made. All one can do is think first, and then proceed with what is most moving. And as you move forward, you will see that the vast majority of things that have happened in your life is a direct result of some choice you've previously made.

Why are you 38 and not married yet? Because you choose not to make getting married a priority. Why do you have high blood pressure, diabetes, and sleep apnea at age 40? Because you choose to continue to eat unhealthy foods and not exercise regularly, and not keep your weight at a reasonable level. Why aren't your children well behaved? Because you didn't, and haven't, established boundaries for them, nor have you been consistent with rule enforcement. Why do you have bad credit? Because in the 1980's the Presidents and Wall Street started screwing you over and didn't even ask... or use KY Jelly!! [I was going to throw President Obama in the mix for laughs but I'm partial... very partial! Hey Michelle! Hey!!! Let's go shopping together!!!]

All joking aside, not controlling what you can control (self) and trying to control what you have no control over (others and certain situations) is disastrous.

CHAPTER 5:

AN EMOTIONAL ENEMA

You have been hanging on to that for so long that you've become... well, emotionally constipated... and you need to have an emotional enema.

~*Brigette Hall*

As I began writing this chapter, I am reminded of a very recent conversation I had with a male friend. I will refer to him as Hunter. Hunter, at the time I am writing this chapter, is in his late 40's, attractive, a divorcee, a father and a preacher. During our conversation, he started talking about his 2nd girlfriend. Yes, you read that correctly: his 2nd, s.e.c.o.n.d. girlfriend. Now, as Hunter talked passionately about what "**_had_** happened," I found myself repeating over and over in my mind... "Did he say his 2nd girlfriend?" I was so enthralled over this fact that I found myself asking, "Hunter, how _old_ were you when this happened?" Hunter answered my question and continued to tell his story.

This is horrible to admit, but I sat there unable to listen because I was stuck on the fact that he responded... "...19..." I recall literally shaking my head, blinking in amazement, and looking off into vacancy and thinking "...19! He did not just say 19!" So, again, I rudely interrupted his walk down memory lane and asked the clarifying question, "Did you say you were 19?" Hunter defensively and emphatically responded, "Yes! Just because you are young does not mean that you don't experience love." While I agreed with him, that was not my crux of contention. Little did he know he would soon state the very problem that I had with his rant. He went on to state:

"It's been 30 years since that happened......."

And there it is....

All I could think was... and those are 30 years that you will _never_ get back.

Now before you rush off thinking Hunter is a loser of some sort, he's not. He works hard, has decent credit, doesn't live with his mother, has his own place, goes to church religiously (even before he accepted his calling), is physically fit, and is quite the gentleman. He simply experienced hurt as a young developing man and made the decision to be _more careful_ where he placed his heart. And had he, by his own admission, been more open about these feelings with another woman he felt deeply for, he would not have met (he feels) all the different women that he has met… including me. Why? He would have been married… years ago. (Sounds like justification to me… but that's another book.)

He continued to talk and I continued to think… "19!? ….. 30 years!?" I recall saying to him, "Hunter, I don't even remember what was going on when I was 19!" How in the world do you hold on to something, anything other than a house, for thirty years?

Unfortunately, this is not an uncommon story. I did, in fact, tell him he is not the only one, male or female, who has held on to past… and passed… hurtful situations for years on end. This is one reason why so many people have only one child… the emotional pain surrounding the failed relationship. This is why there are so many single parent households; people refuse to dive into relationships and open themselves up for the possibility of a good thing. Unfortunately, and fortunately, I cannot say that I am one of these people who can fully understand his plight but I did appreciate him sharing it with me.

I share his story because, as previously mentioned, many men and women are still hanging on to old hurts. Then, without letting go of the past, they refuse to pick one, continuously sleeping around and having "surface" relationships with her, her, and her, or him, him, and him. They go through life hurt, wounded and limping around trying to justify their deviant behaviors. And many of these people are Christians.

How does this happen? How can someone claim to completely and totally believe in some "being" they cannot see, a "being" that is *all* powerful, *all* mighty, *all* knowing, yet they refuse to give their pains to the "being" they <u>completely</u> and totally believe in... who is supposedly able to take all those pains away? (It's ok. I had to read it twice myself... and I wrote it!)

Indeed, how is that possible? What is this problem about? Aren't Christians supposed to be able to go to God, the Supreme Being, and give Him all of their cares? Doesn't the Bible instruct one to cast all their cares on Him because He cares? And yet, they hang on... to pain? How is this? Why is this? Then... why believe? These are very valid questions that many non-believers ask.

Trust Me

The answer to this spiritual conundrum phenomenon came to me one day as I was having one of my infamous meltdowns on my Facebook status. Part of what I wrote is as follows:

I need to know if anyone else is "going through something" other than me.... Some days I can wear the smile you see... but some days it's a struggle. I am NOT talking about those of you who have a "summer home"... I'm talking about those who have lost everything but their mind...and that seems to be slipping too.

As several people responded and the dialog went to discussing faith, one of those people who responded was my cousin, Nastascia. Part of what she wrote was:

That's the thing about faith... everything is not always clear but it works. When we started our business we didn't know how, what, when etc. All we knew is we are gonna have to trust God because change has to happen now. ... I said all that to say this. You may not understand all the details so stop trying. When times get rough, because they will, [you] just enter into a mode of praise and worship knowing that better days are ahead. In all thy ways acknowledge Him and he shall direct your path. Stop wondering when it will happen and just know that it shall happen and ask God for strength to see you through.

After I read these words, I was reminded of how completely my oldest daughter trusts me and values my opinion. It was as if all at once God opened up my understanding of why I was being the fretful and anxious child, and why so many Christians cannot give their pain to Him completely. TRUST, or lack thereof.

See, of my three children, Tamiyra has, well, been with me the longest. As the oldest child, she watched how I operated, heard me walking the floor praying many nights when I was unemployed and money was short, and was the first one to leave home having been fully indoctrinated with many Brigette-isms.

Tamiyra knows that if I say I'm going to do something, it's as good as already being done. She also knows that if I cannot come through on my original plans, I will let her know. She knows that I will "never leave her nor forsake her." Why? She has invested much time in just watching me and me only; listening to me and only me. And because she has watched me and listened to me, she knows me. And since she knows me, she trusts me. **And this is how we come to trust God.**

As I explained to my cousin, I (and many others) am often like that bratty child in the backseat of the car asking repeatedly, "Are we there yet? Are we there yet? I need to lie down! I need to potty! I'm hungry! How much longer!???"

Then there are those children, like my Tamiyra, that will ride the entire way, not say a word, and simply watch everything. Additionally there are those children, like my Lisa and my Michael, whom are so pure in heart and so trusting of the driver that they fall right to sleep... FULLY TRUSTING the person in the driver's seat.

As I write this, I am reminded of where my trust issues started and why I have difficulty fully trusting "the driver."

Again, it started in my childhood around the time all of the other madness was happening.

Aunt Goldie had a terrible habit of falling asleep when she was driving. If I had been asleep, I would be startled awake by the jerking of the car as she swerved to get back into her lane. For a person that doesn't like thrill rides, then or now, this is a most frightening predicament.

We could be going only from Crockett to Lufkin... only 46 miles... and she would fall asleep! Those 46 miles back then consisted of a 2-lane highway with winding curves through the Davy Crockett forest. And she had the unmitigated gall to fall asleep... with me *and* my precious baby sister in the car!! Deer would jump out of those wooded lands... and she had the nerve to fall asleep behind the wheels of a deadly weapon!

Aunt Goldie wasn't much of a radio listener, so she would begin singing in an attempt to keep herself awake. She even invented a game called "Zap and Zip" (see a cow yell "zap"...see a horse yell "zip") for my sister and me to play. I thought she was trying to keep us entertained. Now I know it was her clever way of keeping *herself* awake and alert! A very smart and clever woman she was.

It is simply by Grace that we were never injured nor had a wreck. When it happened, falling asleep behind the wheel, one time too many, she began to stop at Hadid's (a mom and pop grocery) to get some traveling snacks. She would drive and we would feast on Cheetos, Fritos, summer sausage, cheese, Ginger Snaps and Sprite! By then, however, the additional fear and distrust and anxiety had already been established. Thus, it was and still is very difficult for me to "enjoy the ride" if someone else is driving... including God.

Many of you are just like me. Maybe the fear and lack of trust didn't begin with a 46 mile trip down a winding, wooded, deer infested 2-lane highway. Maybe it began with you being molested by a family member or watching your mother get abused. Maybe it began with being raped by your ex-boyfriend.

Maybe it began after being picked on and picked over in high school. Wherever it started, when it comes to trusting God- a being we cannot see- and allowing Him to take the steering wheels of our lives... and when life (the car if you will) starts to swerve, we begin to panic and start asking all these questions (hey Phillip and Emmanuel Hudson) because we are simply trying to .... keep............... GOD..................... *awake*!
Yup! Awake!

God has given us examples of why we can trust Him in His Word. David tells us:

"Behold, he that keepeth Israel shall neither slumber nor sleep. The LORD is they keeper: the LORD is they shade upon they right hand. The sun shall not smite thee by day, nor the moon by night. The LORD shall preserve thee from all evil: he shall preserve thy soul. The LORD shall preserve thy going out and they coming in from this time forth, and even for evermore." Psalm 121: 4-8.KJV.

And in a different version:

Indeed, he who watches over Israel never tires and never sleeps. The LORD himself watches over you! The LORD stands beside you as your protective shade. The sun will not hurt you by day, nor the moon at night. The LORD keeps you from all evil and preserves your life. The LORD keeps watch over you as you come and go, both now and forever." NLT version.

God doesn't need our help to keep Him awake. He is not a man and doesn't require the needs of an invented game to keep him alert and awake. He just needs us to spend time with Him and watch Him as intently and observantly as Tamiyra watched me. Quietly. Not saying a word; just taking it all in. Therefore, when those perfect storms start raising in our lives, we are able to not fret and simply fall soundly asleep, like Lisa and Michael.

Talking to the Mirror

As a preteen, I struggled with my looks. I continued to be the tallest person in my classes. I was dark-skinned when it wasn't popular to have a dark skin complexion. I was always in the classes with "the smart people." I was still one of the best dressed, frequently wearing brands my classmates could only look at in the magazines. I was an outsider.

One day as I walked down our hallway towards the kitchen, Aunt Goldie noticed I was walking with my shoulders slumped. "What are you slouching for? Don't you know women get paid to be tall?"

She sat me down and began to talk to me about her experiences growing up poor, tall, and awkward. She told me about enjoying sports and being competitive and how that was frowned upon when she was younger. She shared with me that she loved to whistle and climb trees and how her Uncle Judge always told her she would never be anything because she could whistle "Dixie!" She also told me how she came to the conclusion that she may not have been the most beautiful female that she knew, but she also knew she "damned sure" wasn't the ugliest female either. She said she realized that she was "okay."

As I sat there listening to her story, tears began to fall. She would go on to tell me that I may not have been able to fully see or understand at that moment, but one day, the very people that were making fun of me would want to be my friend, date me, hell, be like me. Then she told me to go get myself "together" and walk tall.

I went to the bathroom and I stood there looking at my reflection in the mirror. At twelve, I studied my eyes, my skin, my hair, lips, nose and I said, *"You know what Brigette. You may not be the most beautiful person in the world, but you damned sure ain't the ugliest either. You are okay."*

From that moment, from telling myself that I was ok with myself, my self-esteem began to heal and grow. I began to let go of all my anxieties about not fitting in, about being too tall, too dark, too smart, too jazzy and too different. I was okay with being okay. I was okay with being me.

Now it's **your** turn. At some point, you will find yourself in front of a mirror. It is my hope that you will look at yourself really good and talk to your reflection in the mirror. As you brush your teeth and search for any new pimples or age spots or grey hair or wrinkles, it is my hope that you will open your mouth and say... ***"I may not be the most beautiful person I know but I damned sure ain't the ugliest! I am... okay."***

And you are okay. *You* are okay. And guess what... it's really okay to be okay. I mean, who really wants to be Halle Berry anyway? She has stalkers, serious relationship drama *and* a child that's not even in elementary school!

Writing to Release

For this concept, I would like to give credit to the person that this idea therapeutic activity originated from. I do not recall where I first read about this concept, but I do know it was many years ago. Writing can be very therapeutic. In my case, it is a tool that, once I found it, I would use from time to time.

Writing to get something off of your chest is different from journaling. By journaling you want to remember. Writing when you're upset, or better yet pissed off to the highest point of pissedtivity, is not meant to be kept or reviewed at a later date. It is meant to allow you to say things you would *like to* say to someone but you know it may do more harm than good. So you release the fury on paper and then… let that shit go… forever… by burning it, shredding it, or destroying it in some other form.

The idea is to take a mental and verbal dump on paper. And just like you dispose of bio-waste, you dispose this mental waste by some act that prohibits it from returning. Therefore, writing and balling the paper into a wad does not help or work. You can simply pick the wad of paper back up and read it. Taking a mental and verbal dump on paper requires you to burn it or shred it to completely destroy those toxins.

I remember using this technique shortly after I entered college. I refused to allow my daughter to go to day care, or to spend too much time with anyone other than me or one of my aunts. It wasn't until one day I heard a voice inside my head say, "Brigette, you are not your mother."

It was at that point that I realized that I was so intent on my daughter not feeling abandoned as I had felt for much of my life, I was also smothering her and not allowing her to become the individual that she was meant to be. I had to… in a sense… let her go. I had to allow my child to develop her own identity, individuality, and seek her own path.

The thing that I learned most during this point in my life was the difference between being a mother and being a parent. A mother is forever concerned about the welfare of her child. She is concerned about the child's protection, safety, growth and development. But a parent is concerned with the child being whole and being able to positively contribute to society. Many women focus so much on being a good mother, they neglect becoming a good parent. It is my personal belief that this imbalance contributes to hindering children in reaching their full potential because mother never stopped mothering. This is often the root cause of so many people becoming underachievers.

After coming to this realization, I happened to read a book, which I do not recall the title of, that said writing a letter and then burning the letter was helpful in moving beyond tragic events. For my life, I don't remember what that book was titled. Nevertheless, I wrote a long, long, detailed letter to my mother. In that letter I discussed all of my frustrations with her not playing a more active, even if distant, role in my upbringing.

I wrote about not understanding why she didn't send me birthday, Christmas, Easter, or just because cards. I explained to her the emptiness I felt inside caused by not knowing who my father was and where I come from. I wrote and I wrote. I cried and I cried. And then, I burned it. This is the first time in over twenty years that I've actually and actively thought about that letter and its contents. Writing it and burning it brought me much needed relief from my emotional constipation.

Now it's your turn. Find some notebook paper, a paper sack, computer paper, or whatever and write a letter to that person you feel has wronged you. I'm talking about that person, or those persons, that you continually think of and feel that their actions or inactions contributed to your emotional constipation.

As you write, hold nothing back. Write as if you are talking directly to that person and they are unable to respond because you have duct taped their mouth shut! Write recklessly! Write passionately! Write as if your life depends on those words that are coming forward! Use vulgarities! DON'T HOLD BACK! Say exactly what you have always wanted to say but either never had the opportunity or felt too embarrassed. Don't think about it! Just write!

And when you are done writing that letter filled with passion and anger

....

....

....
....
....burn it.
That's right. Burn it and watch it burn.

As you sit there watching it burn, take several slow, deep breathes. Inhale the liberty you will surely feel and as you exhale, release all of that negative energy with every flame, with every ember that is floating away into the universe.

Trust me. I know this may seem a little "out there" but it worked for me and countless others. The Universe is very able to handle all of those deadly toxins you've been carrying around for countless months and years. And The Universe can and will transform those toxins into something beautiful and precious. Just as plants need the carbon dioxide we exhale, they return to us what is both suitable and needed for us to live. So give The Universe the waste.

And when you are done letting it go... Get up. Turn around. And walk away.

What are you waiting on? The next chapter isn't going anywhere. Go!

Write!

Release!

CHAPTER 6:

RELEASE BRINGS RELIEF

Rubbing Each Other's Back

Renew, release, let go. Yesterday's gone. There's nothing you can do to bring it back. You can't "should've" done something. You can only DO something. Renew yourself. Release that attachment. Today is a new day!

~ Steve Maraboli

During the four year period of 1976-1980, I had also begun taking piano lessons twice a week in Grapeland, about a 15 minute drive from Crockett. My music teacher was named Mae Shivers Leaves. Mama Mae, as we called her, just happened to be the first cousin of Mrs. Maggie, my kindergarten teacher assistant. Although my grandmother was an outstanding pianist, she refused to teach me because she felt she would be too hard on me. This used to upset Aunt Goldie to no end! Nonetheless, my grandmother said no but offered assistance when I practiced. And I hated practicing. Looking back at those moments, I agree with my grandmother; she definitely would have been way harder on me than necessary.

Throughout these four years, I had begun to get settled in… somewhat. By now, my oldest aunt had graduated from high school, gone to college, gotten married, had a little girl and named her Nastascia, and moved back to Crockett. I was now old enough to walk across the train tracks with my sister in tow to visit with my twin aunts.

The twins were getting ready to graduate from high school and go to Sam Houston State University in Huntsville. We would sit on the porch and played *Speed*- a card game- and talking about our dreams, walk to Kountry Korner or Adler's. That was a long summer… and the last time I would sit on my grandparents' porch playing speed.

As I entered into 3rd grade, I was now combing my own hair. Sometime during that year, my now 4 yr. old sister decided that I would comb her hair as well. Aunt Goldie was 64 years old by then and "old Arthur," referring to arthritis, was taking its toll on her hands. Up until she graduated and moved away, my oldest aunt, Iwilda, had taken on the responsibility of combing my hair every day before she or I went to school or church. Aunt Goldie would often laugh at the fact that she could not make a straight part to put my hair in ponytails to save her life. And it didn't help that I was very tender-headed as well.

By now, my sister and I had developed a very close relationship. At 4 years old, she knew and understood that Aunt Goldie was not our mother but that I was her sister. Aunt Goldie was very clear about not allowing us to call her mother.

Although I knew who our mother was, my sister had no remembrance of her. I can only imagine what my sister went through mentally as she came to the understanding that her friends had a mama but she did not.

As youngsters, we never talked about the fact that everybody else had a mama and a daddy until it was parents' night at school. I don't know if she felt alone or embarrassed as I did. But I do know that she too felt abandoned, although at this time we didn't know what to call it. So we always stuck together... we had this bond. And wherever I went, she went. And whatever I did, she did. At age 5, she would also begin playing the piano. She liked practicing because I would show her the notes.

As sisters often do, we shared a bathroom and a bedroom. On one particular day, I remember my sister sitting on the toilet and she was having a difficult time. She and I had been having this conversation about God only knows what, and I noticed tears coming from her eyes.

I immediately started rubbing her back and continued talking to her. My great grandmother, Eddie Smith, had done that to me a time or two when I visited her in Tyler. Although I didn't understand it then, I was being supportive of my sister's "efforts" without imposing on *her process*.

So, this would start a trend with my sister and me... rubbing each other's back. When I thought of a subtitle for this chapter, rubbing each other's back seemed to naturally follow. When people experience discomfort of any kind, even after taking medication, being touched or massaged has the tendency to bring comfort… and release.

After holding on to painful memories for so long, sometimes we need someone there to share as we release and let go of all that… shit… literally and figuratively. That individual, however, needs to be capable of understanding that *your* shit is **_your_** shit! They need to understand that they are not the one on the toilet seeking release and relief.

Additionally, they need to be able to endure the smell without making you feel uncomfortable or embarrassed about a naturally occurring cleansing process. They simple need to rub your back and provide supportive banter.

Not everyone is capable of doing this. Many times we find ourselves surrounded by people who say they are our friends and want what is best for us but are often harboring envy in their hearts. These people, emotionally constipated themselves, *really* wish they could sing like you, write like you, dance like you, think like you, have the things you have. I know there are times we've all made the statement, "Oooo if I could do that, you couldn't tell me nothing!" And that's precisely why you can't!. The people of whom I speak definitively have "*a feeling of* **discontent** *and* **resentment** *aroused by and in conjunction with a desire for the possessions or qualities of*" you.

Despite the fact that you have no control over how these people feel, you can control you: what you say and how you respond to them. Always remember that any human being that is envious of another human being is emotionally constipated. Plain and simple. We are all imperfect and we all know humans are imperfect. And just as Michael understood half of the situation and Tamiyra didn't understand the socks would be hidden, these people are operating in limited knowledge and vision.

I am not saying not to trust these people. No. That would be counter this book. What I am saying is, you have control of only you and what you say, what you do and what you think. If you have seen several indicators that someone is envious of you, don't withdraw from them. Just tell them they need… or better yet, purchase them their own copy of *An Emotional Enema*.

Since everyone is not capable of doing this (being supportive of your efforts without imposing on your process)… and you don't have anyone in your circle capable of being that support, seek the help and guidance of a psychologists or mental health expert. These people have been trained to rub the backs of those needing to take or actively taking a dump. They are accustomed to the smells of all kinds of shit.

A good therapist, like Angela Hopkins, MA, of Houston, TX, will give you exercises to practice in order to help loosen those muscles and soften those toxins. If you are budget conscious, a self-help book is just as good as going to a therapist but it takes much more discipline.

Does therapy work? It depends… on you. Does self-help work? It depends… on you. I am only making a suggestion because sometimes… sometimes, talking to someone who doesn't know you (or reading someone else's thoughts through the self-help path) and listening to what they have to say (or doing what is suggested in their book) can be very eye opening. If your goal is to get relief, find what works for you: laxative or enema. Whichever you choose, you will undoubtedly feel better.

Just as having a physical bowel movement requires the expansion and contraction of the rectal muscle, relieving yourself of emotional waste will require similar effort and working on your conscience awareness and your thoughts. Contrary to microwave technology, emotional cleansing and healing does not happen in the time you can heat up a cup of coffee or pop a bag of popcorn. I repeat: Emotional cleansing and healing does not happen in the time you can heat up a cup of coffee or pop a bag of popcorn.

No. Depending on… how backed-up you are, the journey can be both a very long and very painful process. But don't give up! You WILL feel so much better once you've gotten that release. Additionally when you are getting that physical and emotional release, there is a tendency to clench up and attempt to continue holding on to these very things you **know** are causing you pain and are trying to seek release from. Again, the releasing process can and will be very painful. Letting go is very, very, very difficult.

You feel the need to let go and you have the urge to push… but that pain. That pain stops you dead in your tracks. Unfortunately, there is no easy way around this. There is no quick fix. There is no little blue pill.

I wish there were. I liken this pain to that of childbirth; that is very painful, indeed! But once it is over, you have a beautiful new creation. And the joy you feel after you have given birth is of no comparison to all the pain you went through as you labored to see and hold your child. Therefore, you have to determine in yourself that you are going to let it go… that you are going to get rid of all that emotional waste Malcolm X style… "By any means necessary!"

By releasing all those constipated emotions, we open our worlds up to receive the very best the Universe has to offer. Additionally we can become examples for others who are striving to achieve their own emotional release. I will close this chapter with a quote from my friend:

"We NEVER know what the Universe/God has in store for lives that come to be. Life is ironic like that. Being a powerful example personally seems to be the best leverage one can attain. And it puts us in a place where we have the energy to respond to difficult situations." - Jeff Owens

CHAPTER 7:

FLUSHING IT ALL AWAY-

LET THAT SH*T GO

Some people believe holding on and hanging in there are signs of great strength. However, there are times when it takes much more strength to know when to let go and then do it.

~ Ann Landers

*A*s I began developing this chapter, I recalled a line from *Love Jones*, "...just let it go and walk away." While pondering over the powerful meaning in these seven words, I visualized a person standing on a street corner, holding onto a signpost. The light turns green, they let go of the signpost and walk across the street. After arriving on the other side of the street, the pedestrian *looks back* at the signpost they previously let go of and decides to walk *back* across the street to grab hold of the old signpost *again*. Across the street they go. After being there for a while, they tire and decided to walk to the other side of the street again. And again, after getting to the other side of the street, they *look back* and decide to walk *back* across the street to the original signpost. They continue to do this repeatedly... holding onto the signpost then, for whatever reason, they tire, decide to let it go... walk a short distance across the street only to turn around and go right back to that same... signpost... they had previously let go of.

If you can imagine someone actually doing this for a long period of time, we can all understand that the person would never get anywhere... except the width of that *one* street corner. Think of all the time wasted on that *one* corner. While the person may meet different people approaching and leaving that corner, the individual never takes the opportunity to venture into the city, exploring and experiencing all the wonderful attractions and learning opportunities it has to offer. This person, by repeatedly making the same, identical choice, limits themself.

That fact of this matter is there are thousands upon thousands of people living their lives the width of a street. Many never venture far from their six block radius or their small towns. And there are those that are thirty and older who have never completely left the safety net of home. These people often use the excuse that they live at home because they are "helping their parents out."

How many of you are guilty of the same behavior? Repeatedly "saying" you have let it go, only to not get very far from that particular thing (person, place, or situation), then turn around and go directly back to that same... signpost. This is not progress. This is fear personified. Think for moment... have you been guilty of this same behavior?

If you have been in a relationship for years on end and have yet to see any progress in the relationship, you have more than likely succumbed to this signpost fiasco. You get tired of standing there on that corner, holding that signpost, decide to let go, move a short distance away, only to turn around and walk that short distance back to that same old signpost. A more commonly known term to describe the same behavior is "the slot machine effect."

The slot machine effect results from recognizing you should get out of the relationship you are in, but choosing to not only stay but to continue making deposits even though you are getting *no* returns. You continue telling yourself: "It's gonna pay off! I know it's going to pay off. I've put too many quarters in this machine for it *not* to pay off and pay big! Come on! Big money!"

Unfortunately, you don't even get small change.

Since you have put an enormous amount of time, effort, and money into this relationship, you keep looking and hoping for a big payoff but... it never comes. You court the idea of leaving, of letting go and walking away, but because you fear that someone else will come along, put in one quarter and hit it big, you remain in that relationship subjecting yourself to repeated un-fulfillment, blatant disrespect and emotional turmoil, yet obtaining nothing in return but a tired back and hurting ass.

Allow yourself to get some relief by flushing away those things over which you have no control. You have already taken that royal dump… so why are you standing there looking inside the toilet, trying to figure out some way to make it smell more fragrant? Why are you standing there looking at that turd trying to figure out how you can hold on to it a little longer?

Wipe your ass, throw in the tissue, and hit the lever! Let that sh*t go!!!!!! Let it go… and walk away. A recent post from Inspirational Quotes to Live & Learn said it this way:

"Always know when to let go. When a thought is bringing you more misery than peace, let go of the thought. When a person is bringing you more miser than joy, let go… You cannot be your best if you lack joy and peace in your life…"

Let me be clear. YOU CAN ONLY CHANGE AND CONTROL YOU! You can no more change a person than you can change the initial stench of manure. And let me open your mind to something revolutionary: even after the smell has faded from the manure… *manure is still manure*… Shit is still… shit.

Flushing the Right Stuff

I am reminded of a recent conversation I was having with a friend of mine. I was telling her how, for the life of me, I couldn't understand how people put on airs and become one way in public, but in private… at home… they are completely the opposite. She lashed out at me telling me that I needed to let it go because *I* can't change the individual. She stated that this particular person would be dead and gone, and I would be angry because *I* hadn't let it go.

Her thoughts and comments made me wonder if this situation was an area of emotional constipation for me. She mentioned that I always talk about it… and admittedly I do… because I'm one such person that is quite the same in public as I am at home. (I'm almost exactly the same…almost.) However, after some rapid mental digging, I determined that her comments didn't *quite* fit what I was talking about concerning this particular person.

I explained to her I wasn't angry at or trying to change the person. I honestly wanted to understand this particular person, a close family member, and others with this same type of behavior. I really would like to understand how parents can have more than one child and give preference to one child and not the other. That whole "Jacob have I loved but Esau have I hated" thing.

While I understand the Biblical symbolism of the above mentioned, I am yet to understand how parents will do for one child and not do the same thing for the other child. I'm not talking about using different methods of punishment, because all people, children included, respond differently and need different methods of communicating and disciple. I'm not talking about them not knowing about a situation because the child did not share the need. Let me paint you a picture.

I want to understand how a parent can have three children, let's say triplets, in college, and will give one child money for books yet refuses to give the other two children money for books. And yes, they have enough money to go around for the other two children. I'm talking about will fill up the gas tank in one child's car but will flat out refuse to fill the other children's cars. And constantly and consistently shows favoritism towards one child and shuns the other two. That... I do not understand.

Furthermore, I'm talking about people who go to work/church/public, give one hundred percent effort at work/church/public, are kind and friendly at work/church/public... but as soon as they get home, behind those closed doors, they become bitter, anger, mean... just outright cantankerous! And, no, it has nothing to do with them being tired... because as soon as a non-member of their private, inner circle comes around, they become *that* person at work/church/public.

This also has nothing to do with the home being untidy, the spouse being un-anything. It has to do with them presenting one persona in public and a Mr. Hyde persona at home. Completely disingenuous. I, like many others, do not understand this or these type people. Fakes, they are commonly called; but I personally believe there is something more to this personality flaw than the eye can see. Dr. Phil... I'm sure you have more insight on this personality type, so let's discuss this over coffee! Help me understand!

My point: it's one thing to not fully understand a thing and to seek out more knowledge and a better understanding. Take statistics. You don't stop trying to gather a working knowledge of it because it tends to have so many layers to uncover before you get to the solution. You continue to work at it until you have at least a basic understanding of the steps and how the answer was calculated.

However trying to *change* a person... an adult person no doubt, trying to get your husband to eat rice pudding when he has already told you and shown you that he doesn't like it... that's no good. Let that shit go. Trying to get your wife to play tennis after she has already said she doesn't like competitive sports... es no bueno. Trying to make your family member get off drugs when they have already expressed, in word and action, they have no desire to stop; no good. Let it go.

When they reach the point that they are tired of carrying around all of the emotional waste, they will seek out a means to detox. They will find a method to facilitate their own emotional enema. Again, let them handle their own shit.

Practice what you preach

Let That Sh*t Go! West

I would like to take a moment and talk about "church folk." Since I am on the subject of understanding how people show favoritisms, it follows that we discuss the seemingly forgotten Golden Rule: *Do unto others as you would have the do unto you*... treat people how you want to be treated in return. And this leads me to "church folk."

Having been raised in the church and having a strong relationship with the only Father I know, I am baffled. There are so many "church folk" that attend every single service the church offers, sing in the choir, usher on the hospitality committee, and teach Sunday School. However, when it comes to being a *Good Samaritan* and put into practice what they claim they believe, teach and value... crickets.

I remember a time when my car was down. The timing chain had broken and, a single parent at the time, I was unable to immediately get it repaired. I was living in South Austin and many members of the church I attended at the time lived in North Austin. I can count on one hand how many people were willing to take me home... and gas wasn't nearly as high as it is now... even with me offering to give them money for gas ... and we had just gotten out of church! How does *that* happen?

I would repeatedly hear, "Oh... I live north. Or, I'm not going that way." Very few times would someone go out of their way, like my friend Lila Beasley Murray, and go above and beyond offering assistance. Yes, we could say that I shouldn't have expected someone to help me... and I didn't. I took the bus many nights without ever asking. Nevertheless, as I thought about the beliefs, professions, and confessions of our Faith, I wondered how often one passes up the opportunity to exemplify and live out church doctrine in real time on their way to and from... the church house.

My good friend, and brother, Aaron Smith, Sr. is another such person. A few years ago he shared with me an opportunity that came his way to practice what he preaches... literally. At this particular time, he had recently received the 501c3 designation for his not-for-profit organization Outside the Pulpit Ministries (OTPM) and was busy trying to provide assistance to people in need.

A family, previously displaced by Hurricane Katrina, was now living in the Austin area. Through various channels they found their way to OTPM. On this occasion, OTPM had been called for a simple request of providing gas for their vehicle. Aaron tells them where to meet him, they get there, and they start the gas pump.

While the gas was pumping, they strike up a small conversation but the young man interrupts and asks, "You want me to stop it?" The reply is... No. Let it keep running. They continue to talk and after another moment or so, the passenger, who was sitting in the car, asks "Do you want him to stop it?" The reply, again, is... No. Let it keep running. The passenger asks, "Are you sure? It's going to cost a lot to fill this tank up..." Aaron reassured them it was fine. When the pump stopped, less than $60 dollars later, the young man was in awe. He stated that no one had *ever* filled their tank. Nobody. One tank of gas... One tank of gas made a difference in someone's life.

What does this story have to do with flushing it all away? We must learn to let go of the things that we have no control of, learn how to move forward, learn to ask for help with things that are too heavy to carry alone, and let the past go. In this situation, they had been displaced by a natural disaster and had to do the only thing they could do... rebuild their lives.

Are you practicing what you preach? This one tank of gas was nothing but a seed in this young man's life, but assuredly was a sign of hope and of better things to come. If my memory serves me correctly, the young man was not yet 22, and he and his mother and siblings had escaped the deadly clutches of Katrina with only their lives. They had obtained housing and other resources to help piece their lives back together. Yet, no one had ever provided them with a full tank of gas. Until OTPM.

If you were to begin now, doing what you can and controlling what you can… which is you… what will be some of the things you let go of? Are you dogmatically trying to do it all by yourself because you have depended on people in the past and they let you down? Have you closed yourself off and are now living in a world of isolation and seclusion? How are you blocking someone who desperately wants to plant a seed of hope inside of you? What opportunities of change are you missing out on? Where is your tank of gas? Church folks, are you being a living example of the *Good Samaritan*?

Determine now that you are going to allow yourself to be completely filled with a full tank of gas. You have emptied yourself of all the toxic wastes you have held on to for far too long. Empty from taking *An Emotional Enema*, you are now ready to be filled with new ideas, new experiences, new relationships, and new opportunities.

Imagine all the places you can go (shout out to Dr. Seuss- may he rest in peace) with a full source of energy… a full tank of gas! But remember, BEFORE you can be filled with a new source of energy you first have to leave that corner and let all that past shit go.

Renewed Energy

Imagine that you are now operating with a full tank of gas and have accepted that you cannot make another grown person do anything. You've let the toxins of control go. You now understand that you can only make suggestions. And you now understand that suggestions do *not* have to be taken. You fully receive that you *cannot* and will not change another grown person or their behaviors you feel are undesirable.

You now understand that they control themselves and they are responsible for their own individual choices. Not you. Them. You understand that some things do not have anything to do with you or your love for them. You accept that you can provide support when *they* initiate the change. You understand your position and can now *encourage* them... now you can rub their back. You now accept that they have to let go of their own shit... They have to have their own personal bowel movement and have to have their own personal emotional enema.

You cannot make them rush their releasing process. You accept that you cannot make them leave the Katrina's of life; the torrential storms life throws their way. And if they attempt to draw you into their constipated emotions, you can decide to walk away... to save you. You can decide to... let it go and walk away! You have your tank full of gas and, while you are happy to carpool, you are aware that everyone has to buckle up for their own safety, wear their own seatbelt, or pay their own fine.

Flushing it all Away

This is not to say that people do not change. They do. That's one of the beautiful things about human beings: we change. People do grow up. People do mature. People come to understand that there are no mistakes in life, only choices... both good choices and bad ones. People learn how to make better choices. And people *make* better choices. But when these changes happen, it has to be a choice that originates from within the individual. If it does not come from within, no permanent change really occurs.

I have a friend that used to suck her thumb. It was a habit that began when she was a child and, although her family members tried everything they could to make her stop, it never changed. In 1995, she began working in a day care center and, since she would be with infants, changing poopy diapers and sucking her thumb gave my friend a bit of cognitive dissonance and anxiety simply from thinking of inadvertently getting poop on her thumb! She had, as my mentor Gigi Bryant and others say, a **BFO**… a *blinding flash of the obvious*! She had to stop sucking her thumb.

After twenty-four and a half years of sucking my thumb, I was able to break myself from the automatic lifting my hand to my mouth behavior in six months. It took another six months to completely stop having the thumb craving all together. Hi. My name is Brigette, and I sucked my thumb… for years!

Believe it or not, thumb sucking is a very addictive habit. I didn't realize how much control it had over my life until I decided to stop. Indeed, giving up my thumb sucking habit was the hardest thing I have had to do. Once I decided to take a "no more" stance and began to actively stop sucking my thumb, I noticed, little by little, how much more I was able to accomplish because I wasn't busy taking a "thumb-break." And, yes, those are as real as a smoke break!

When I was ready, when I deemed it absolutely necessary for my personal health (because of the unsettling poop thoughts) I… I… changed… my own… behavior.

You cannot change your past. You cannot change how you were raised. You cannot change your parents' poor decisions. You cannot undo your poor decisions. You cannot change your children's biological father. You cannot bring back that aborted child. You cannot live out missed opportunities.

You cannot erase, redo, or undo any part of your past. You cannot completely undo damage done from sucking your thumb.

You can, however, change your behavior. You can think before you speak. You can be good to yourself. You can look in the mirror and acknowledge that you may not be the best looking person in the world but you damned sure aren't the ugliest.

You can find peace.

You can move beyond that corner. You can find balance.

You can let that shit go!

Rudyard Kipling says it best:

IF

If you can keep your head when all about you
Are losing theirs and blaming it on you;
If you can trust yourself when all men doubt you,
But make allowance for their doubting too:
If you can wait and not be tired by waiting,
Or, being lied about, don't deal in lies,
Or being hated don't give way to hating,
And yet don't look too good, not talk too wise;
If you can dream---and not make dreams your master;
If you can think---and not make thoughts your aim,
If you can meet with Triumph and Disaster
And treat those tow impostors just the same:
If you can bear to hear the truth you've spoken
Twisted by knaves to make a trap for fools,
Or watch the things you gave your life to, broken,
And stoop and build 'em up with worn-out tools;
If you can make one heap of all your winnings
And risk it on one turn of pitch-and-toss,
And lose, and start again at your beginnings,
And never breathe a word about your loss:

Let That Sh*t Go!   West

If you can force your heart and nerve and sinew
To serve your turn long after they are gone,
And so hold on when there is nothing in you
Except the Will which says to them: "Hold on!"
If you can talk with crowds and keep your
virtue,
Or walk with Kings---nor lose the common touch,
If neither foes nor loving friends can hurt you,
If all men count with you, but none too much:
If you can fill the unforgiving minute
With sixty seconds' work of distance run,
Yours is the Earth and everything that's in it,
And---which is more---you'll be a Man, my son!

You can choose to embrace your past. You can choose to learn from the past. You can choose to grow from poor decisions. You can choose to forgive those who have hurt you. You can choose to wipe, toss, and flush away all the toxic waste held in your emotions. And when you do… please don't forget to wash your hands.

CHAPTER 8:

CLEANSING-

WASH YOUR HANDS PLEASE

You can't hold on to water. It fills you up but never stays. It's only good to wash away, today.

~ Cheryl Cole

This was the most difficult chapter for me to write. Talking about physical cleansing is not something many people openly discuss. And although this book discusses emotional health, to press home the importance of taking care of our emotions, I had to first touch on the physical realm.

My journey took me to an upscale mall in the Seattle area. As I pretended to put on mascara, I reflected on being in a public restroom, what we all do in the restroom stalls and I began making observations. I observed something very disturbing. Very, very, very, very, very, very, very few women wash their hands after releasing and relieving themselves. (*__long dramatic pause__*)

GROSS!!!!

And I'm sure you men have the same nasty habit! Based on the restroom scene in Ben Stiller's movie "Along Came Polly" (Hey Ben!!!) … you do. However, since no one in my circle wanted to stand in the men's room and collect data for me, I can't concretely say it happens. So Ladies…

WE MUST DO BETTER!

It appeared that late teens and college-aged females were the worst culprits! Busy on their phones, they repeatedly left the restroom without washing the disease carrying germs away. This also made me wonder if they even bothered to wipe at all. Yes, I know that's a gross thought but you were forewarned!

The second group of women that were guilty, repeatedly, of not *thoroughly* washing their hands was middle-aged women. While they did turn the water on and let it run across their fingertips, they did not complete half of a verse of the birthday song. Although water touched their fingers, they, too, were still germy. In too much of a hurry to get back to their IPhone scanning, they made me raise an eyebrow as well.

Very few women I observed washed their hands before and after using the toilet. While some may think that is a bit extreme, when you think about it, washing your hands twice... before and after you do the do... is not a bad practice to begin. Think about it. After all, you did touch that germ infested door handle somewhere and you're about to touch your hoo-haa....? *(Hoo-haa = vagina)*

The two groups I observed that *were* consistent with washing their hands were 1) women with children and 2) women with friends. This really got me to wondering: are women more concerned about the health *of* their children than **being healthy for** their children? And do women really put that much thought into keeping up pretenses so their friends won't know their dirty little secrets?

Being in a hurry gets us nowhere fast except stuck in a ditch. As my celebrity look-and-act-alike India.Arie sings- "... you've got your hands in the air with your feet on the gas..." And if we are in such a hurry that we fail to take care of simple hygiene tasks, what does this say about our overall health? What does this say about us cleansing ourselves physically, mentally and spiritually?

Too often focused on and attending to trivial matters, we neglect to stop and take **twenty seconds** to really purify... our hands! Often in a rush, we sprinkle a little water on the problem and feel we have done it justice. Au contraire mon fraire.

According to the Center for Disease Control (CDC) several diseases and other medical conditions spread because people either do not wash their hands or do not wash their hands properly. Some of these diseases include hepatitis A, salmonella, giardiasis, streptococcus, staphylococcal organisms, and influenza, to name a few. On the CDC website, there are several resources listed including guidance on when and how we are to wash our hands. Of these includes washing your hands before eating food, after touching an animal or its waste and after using the toilet.

When we fail to properly cleanse ourselves we invite, pick up and carry around, on and in our body's (as in physical body, mental body, and spiritual body) all the impurities and toxins that others have left behind.

Unintentionally we "pick up" things throughout the day. Along with germs and other harmful impurities, we pick up dirt and debris, we pick up negativity and bitterness, we literally can and do even pick up… shit. And yet, as we venture throughout our day, we refuse to take **twenty seconds,** much less than half of a minute, to stop and admire the vastness of the sky, the sounds that surround us in stereo, or even to sing, as we wash our hands, the one song that we all know the words to and love to hear sung to us… the Happy Birthday song.

And then we wonder to ourselves why we are so tired, sluggish, and sickly.

Now consider this: how often do you really take the time to purify and cleanse, *thoroughly* washing away, all of the dirt and rubbish you have picked up throughout the day? While you stand in the shower, routinely doing your cleansing regime, how often do you really wash behind your ears and scrub between your toes? Do you actually take the towel and thoroughly rub long enough to kill any odor causing bacteria or do you just let the water run over and through them?

More importantly, how often do you *attend* to what you are actually doing? How often do you think about what your body is capable of doing? How often do you take the time to marvel at the mechanics of your hands, their ability to grasp the shower gel, to squeeze the bottle with just enough pressure as to not squeeze out too much? How often do you focus intently on the ability in your arms to extend up to the roof, the ability to bend your back or lift your leg? How often do these things, things that many of us take for granted daily, fascinate and illuminate you to how blessed you really are?

People with muscular dystrophy, cerebral palsy or sarcoidosis would gladly take your blessing that you often fail to appreciate. Far too often, we hurriedly rush through our days. Likewise we rush through our weeks, months, and yes, our years. As I child, I recall being in a hurry to "grow up." I'm sure the majority of us have been guilty of making that wish. Yet, when we became adult-aged some of us wanted to return to childhood.

While some of us fully embraced adulthood, unfortunately, there are some of us who continued to act as though we were still those careless little toddlers putting our hands on things that could bring us harm and then placing those nasty little phalanges in our mouths without ever considering all of the toxins and waste we would introduce to our bodies... much like leaving the restroom without washing your hands. WASH your hands.
Wash. Your. Hands.

Bathe Your Mind

Another body that needs regular and through cleansing is our mental body. Our *mental hygiene,* as my friend Jeff Owens of Syracuse, New York refers to it, is equally important to achieving overall health. How often do we take the time to wash away impure and unhealthy thinking? Someone referred to negative, unproductive thoughts as "stinking thinking." I found this term to be very fitting for this section. Mental purification should be as much a part of overall hygiene as is taking a daily shower and brushing our teeth.

I cannot stress enough how important the health of our thought and emotional lives are. I have given you example on top of example of how thoughts operate. Our thought life, or our state-of-mind, determines all subsequent actions. Keeping it health is essential to your well-being. But how do you go about cleansing your thoughts?

Below I have listed a few activities I chose to purify my mind. Also listed are the activities my husband and children practice. I hope you will try them and find them as engaging, purifying and as gratifying as we do.

Brigette's Mental Purifiers

My favorite mental hygiene activity is to find the nearest, natural or man-made, large body of water and stare at it. I will go out on the pier or deck and literally just sit and watch the water move. As I focus on the moving water, I think of nothing but the water. I breath in the water, I listen intently to the waves crashing into the pier, and I remain there still and silent, letting the water "wash over" my mind.

Recently, I turned on the shower, lay back in the tub and let the water cascade over my body. I closed my eyes and tried to imagine what it was like to be inside my mothers' womb. I listened to the rhythm of the shower. I thought felt the water pool around my limbs. I let the water "wash over" me.

Another activity I practice is watching the wind blow through the trees. I know you can't actually "see" the wind blowing through the trees, but you can see and feel its presence. I will go to a park, park my car in a shaded area with a view of the trees, and simply sit quietly in my car, roll down the windows just enough to feel the breeze and then watch the branches bend and sway to the blowing wind. As I focus on the sensation of the cool breeze and seeing the branches bend, my negative thoughts, too, are removed with the blowing wind.

Still another activity I would like to share from my mental hygiene kit is listening to children's' laughter. I go to the local mall, find the indoor play area and stand quietly off to the side and watch the little ones run, climb, play, and laugh. There's something about children's' laughter that always invokes a sense of purity and hope.

Other activities that I enjoy but have not actively done in recent days include: gardening (there's nothing like being on your knees in dirt that is more gratifying), trying new receipts for new dishes I find online, getting a full-body message (the power of touch is soooooo amazingly therapeutic), going to the gym, riding around in the car with my female friends, and going to open houses or model homes.

Larry's Mental Purifiers

When I asked my aircraft mechanic husband what activity he used to cleanse his thought pallet, he immediately responded, "I don't do that... I like having dirty thoughts." Typical man answer! Nevertheless, with the shrewdness of Esther, I gained the response I sought.

When my husband needs to purify his mind, he stated he goes to play a few hands of poker. My husband explained that the very nature of poker forces one to change their state of mind. And depending on whether he wins, loses, draws or has some "bad beats" (how you like my poker lingo) he says his mood improves greatly or not so greatly. Nevertheless, his mental purification process benefits him by causing him to move away from the negativity and causing him to refocus on more strategic activities. While this would frustrate me to no end, it helps my husband realign his thoughts, purify his mind, and find his center.

Now I know I have that one group of people that believe that gambling is a sin and will send you straight to hell. The basis for this reasoning is that Jesus apparently went Rambo on some gamblers. Thing is, these particular gamblers where in... The

Temple! Not at the local casino or bingo hall. Nevertheless, if you have a gambling problem, seek professional help.

Tamiyra's Mental Purifiers

Whenever Tamiyra needs to clear her mental space, she gets in what we have termed a "hallelujah cleaning fit (HCF)." During their childhood, I would get them up on Saturday mornings and start them to cleaning. Today, she continues this practice but she cleans EVERYTHING! I'm talking bedroom, bathroom, kitchen, cabinets, windows... everything.

Then she starts throwing away anything in her path that is not bolted to the floor or too heavy to be picked up by a single person. She goes through her closet and starts pulling clothes off hangers. She will go through the pantry and start checking dates! She will throw away tubes of toothpaste that still has a week's worth of toothpaste left! She will take the toilet tissue out of the package and throw the packing away!

After she has thrown away any and everything she has identified as clutter, she begins to wash and will rearrange her bedroom or redecorate her space. While she is in her HCF, she is listening to music. Anything that has an up tempo is on her playlist be it hip-hop, R&B, Gospel, dance hall, or go-go.   And when she has done all of these activities, her mind is free of excess clutter as well. Truly, Tamiyra gets it in.

Lisa's Mental Purifiers

As a full-time student working two different jobs as well as being the occasional babysitter and trying to become a model, in addition to already being "an artist and temperamental," Lisa is presently living a very full life at age twenty.

When I asked her what she did when she needed to purify her mental space, she stated that she goes somewhere to be around people she doesn't know or she takes herself to a movie. If the weather is nice outside, she said she enjoys going to the park or going to sit by the water. (Wonder where she got that from.)

As a child, when Lisa was distressed she would often make her way over into a quiet little area and would diligently play alone until she decided to join the others. Even as small children, our innately given purification mechanisms let us know when we need to take care of self. How unfortunate it is that we lose sight of these truths as we get older and busier. Find your inner child and remember, reclaim, and regroup.

Michael's Mental Purifiers

I've never been a fifteen year old boy, but I have observed that teen boys are under tremendous pressure to "become." And as parents, educators and mentors, we need to ensure that we also help them find and develop ways to care for their mental hygiene. If it's never too young to get emotionally constipated, it surely is never too young to develop a mental hygiene regime. At fifteen, Michael says he enjoys playing basketball alone or lifting weights to cleanse his mind.

One thing I have observed of my son is that he is a bit of a fashonistO! He absolutely loves clothing, shoes, and accessories. This could have something to do with his newly found obsession with females but... that too is another book. I believe, to aide in his mental purification process, he enjoys walking around in the mall. My son is a people person, much like me, and being around people tends to give the mental recharge we sometimes need.

Although they have very different vibes, Westfield Southcenter Mall in Tukwila, Washington and Bellevue Square Mall in Bellevue, Washington are his regular hang outs. With the constant flow, on any given day, of every working class nationality in America and centrally located, Southcenter is quicker and easier for teens to get to using public transportation. Southcenter never fails to have a group of teens representing different nationalities hanging around eating burgers or teriyaki chicken. Having watched them exchange dialog, I've come to the conclusion that these groups of teens are talking about how silly we adults are for not having a more diverse group of friends we can hang out with and enjoy life.

It is my hope that if you have not begun some type of mental hygiene routine, the above has inspired you to take an active role in your mental well-being. We must learn this simple truth: each individual has the duty to take care of self... FIRST. Without caring for self, FIRST, we are in no shape to see to the needs and care of others.

I mean, would you want your doctor operating on you if she were angry at her husband? Would you want to be on a plane knowing that the pilot decided NOT to take his Haldol or lithium? Would you want a dentist pulling your teeth without having practiced first?

Mental hygiene, mental health, a mental purification process are all as equally important as physical hygiene, physical health, and a physical purification process. Take the time today to think about the things that bring you peace and put you in a better mood. Set aside time to enjoy doing whatever that activity is. Go ahead. All this other stuff will be there. Take the time. BATHE your mind.

Soak Your Spirit

The final body, and probably our most important body, is that of our spirit. As my cousin Irma Robinson says, "I believe in a higher power and I choose to call Him God!" You should know by now that I am a Believer. I believe in The Triune Spirit: God the Father, God the Son, and God the Holy Ghost. My intent in this portion of the book is not to attempt to get you to convert to my beliefs, but to encourage you to believe in something greater than man.

Whether you choose to use Yahweh, Jehovah, Universe, Allah, Big Guy, The Man Upstairs... makes me no difference. Many of us are known by different names and yet we are one entity. Tamiyra calls me *mumzy*, Lisa calls me *Nisa's mama*, and depending on how he's feeling, Michael calls me *Mother* or *Moh Dah*. Larry calls me *Brigette Hall*. Really he does. Some of my cousins call me *Bri*. My grandmother called me *Bid* until the day she died (and now my cousins, if they are reading this, know my secretly kept nickname.) People from Crockett call me *Brigette Hopkins*... and yes they say my first AND last name (we do that to EVERYBODY). My friend Howard Green calls me *Lady*. Several of my friends call me *Brig*.

My point? All of these names are directed towards <u>me</u>. Hence, when it comes to taking care our spiritual body, let's not miss a wonderful opportunity to learn something new and grow deeper by getting caught up in religious semantics. HE knows you are talking to HIM! So just talk.

If our physical and mental bodies are subject to becoming dirty, so does our spiritual body. In life, there come those times when no amount of bathing, no amount of tide watching, or no amount of children's laughter will bring you out of the funk you are in. This is often felt during times of tremendous loss; being fired from a job and not regaining employment quickly; repeated rejection from various positions you know you are well qualified for; a divorce, and yes and most often the hardest, the death of a close loved one.

Although my grandmother was very dear to my heart and I miss her very much, nothing compared to the tremendous loss I felt on and after September 27, 2003… the day my Aunt Goldie, died. Although I didn't cry inconsolably, emptiness overtook me. As the nurse rounded the corner saying, "She's a DNR! She's a DNR!" my soul sank to its lowest point. As I uttered the words "Do not resuscitate" to answer my sister's question, I also asked… "Why, Aunt Gold? Why didn't you tell us?"

Later that day, I found myself sitting in the middle of the street, the same street that years earlier I cried in because I was left behind, feeling yet again lost and left alone. I just sat there… looking down the end of the street… wondering… how on earth would I make it through life without the one person that never lied to me (other than about Santa Clause)… the one person that believed in me MORE than I ever believed in myself… the one person that never abandoned me. Waves of the pain of my constipated past kept coursing over my soul. No one will ever stay. No one ever stays. You have been abandoned… once again.

It wasn't until the day of the service that I started seeking cleansing for my soul. As the service director lowered her head down into her solid white casket with gold trim and gold angels on each corner, I felt the uncontrollable urge to stand up. And I did stand, holding myself… and watched. With great pageantry and care, he honored the shell of the woman he had known most of his life in the most beautiful way. As he slowly closed the top of the casket, I continued to hold myself as if to keep me from running away. And with that, my Aunt Goldie was gone. I sat down.

As the service progressed, person after person got up to share some story of how she had an incredible impact on their lives. Person after person spoke such wonderful words of kindness. Yet something was missing. Something did not rest well inside of me. These people, the same people... people who were born and raised and presently lived in Crockett and knew Crockett "business"... seemed... to be....... ignoring............ me? Us?

They would address my grandfather. They would address my... mother? They even addressed my uncles and aunts! But me and the other four members of "The Fabulous Five," the five that my parent had spent the last twenty-eight years of her life raising and providing for... received... nothing. No recognition whatsoever. "What... is... wrong... with... this... picture!?" I thought. This was *our* parent! This was *our* mother! This was *our* father! This was *our* **all**! And we have lost her... and you... you... ignore... us!? You put US in the group with "...the Hopkins... *family*!?"

And then, the most redemptive thing happened. In an amazingly chivalrous manner, Mr. Henry Ford Reese says; "Would Brigette, the oldest of Goldie's five children, come forward and receive this plaque in her honor." I arose from my seat on the second pew. In my jubilee white suit, I walked forward, proud that someone recognized me as being her... child. That BLESSED and CLEANSED my SOUL! I was her child.

Many of you will never be able to full understand why I needed to be recognized as her child. Maybe orphans can because they understand that feeling of not knowing your biological parents. So Mr. Reese recognizing me as her *child* and not just her great-niece purified my soul. Let me try to explain.

Nothing in this world can compare to giving birth, experiencing the childbirth process, or parenthood. NOTHING. Whether you ladies went to the sperm bank or... the club to pick your baby daddy (I don't care if you hate that term...bite me!) or whether you are the Caucasian couple that lives in Eastern Washington and adopted little Esther from Ethiopia, absolutely nothing compares to having your own child. To all of you animal lovers that call your pets your babies... my friend Nicole, who had five... ok four... cats at the time she gave birth to her son, will tell you that giving birth to something that comes from you does not compare to having a pet.

We've all observed how happy children are to see their mother or father whom, most times, they've only been apart from for a few hours. They will run to them and hug them as if their parents are the most important people on earth! The children commence to talking a mile-a-minute, telling them about their exciting day and things they did in their pre-K class... and at recess... and at lunch.

Now the parent(s) could look like a Gila monster, wearing too little flip-flops and a Jeri curl, have thirty-two missing teeth and work at the corner store as the restroom monitor. But to that child, to *their* child, they are as beautiful and elegant as Michelle Obama (yes, I'm shouting out to my First Lady... again!) and as smart, intelligent, and genteel as her husband! (I have no shame.) These children know they belong.

At four years old, I no longer belonged. For over twenty-seven years I was no one's *child*. Sure, I was Coach Hopkins' granddaughter, the twin's niece, Tasha's sister, Tauras, Traye, and Peter's cousin, Shawna's friend, Mama Mae's prized student, a 4-H member, a Girl Scout, the president of the youth choir and drill team, but for twenty-seven years, twenty-seven, I had not *publicly* **belonged** to anyone as their *child*... until that day.

In Abraham Maslow's Hierarchy of Needs theory, belonging is achieved only after physiological (food, water, etc.) and safety needs are met. Also in his theory, this sense of belonging must be achieved before one can begin to develop *healthy esteem* and confidence as well as reach higher levels of achievement and progress further to *self-actualization*, which includes the ability to create, solve problems, and accept facts without prejudice.

After being identified as her child in 2003, I have gone on to complete an undergraduate degree in psychology and graduate degree in business administration, and am presently pursuing a third, a Ph.D. in organizational psychology (which may change to forensic psych)... all while writing this little ditty. There are other things I've accomplished as well since then, but the point is... until I *belonged* I could not... and DID NOT *achieve*.

What does this have to do with your soul? Simple.

Who do you belong to?

CHAPTER 9:
DISINFECT- DIVORCE ANDBEING A CHRISTIAN

I do not consider divorce an evil by any means. It is just as much a refuge for

women married to brutal men as Canada was to the slaves of brutal masters.

~ Susan B. Anthony

There are many, many, many pastors, preachers, teachers, spiritual leaders, religious gurus and the like that do not and will not touch the subject of getting a divorce. Stating that the Bible teaches against divorce, they, therefore feel they also must teach against it. Many do not re-marry divorcees, and some refuse to give counsel to those going through divorce proceedings. Yet, the church house is filled with Believers who absolutely and completely love the Lord but have experienced the harsh reality of divorce. I am such a Believer.

Nevertheless, as a Believer, (*and by Believer I mean one who has accepted Jesus as my personal Savior, believes that He was in the beginning with God, was born of a virgin, came down through 42 generations of Jew descendants, was baptized by John the Baptist, turned water into wine, healed the sick, raised the dead, died on the Cross for my sins and the sins of the world, and rose again on the 3rd day, and is now seated on the right hand of God*), I personally believe that a marriage that began wrong... one that was entered into ill-advised and/or for the wrong reasons (she was pregnant)... is the same as fornicating, stealing, committing adultery, lying, not having faith and all the other sins... a sin that *can be* forgiven and *can be* moved away from... through divorce!

If you went to your pastor with the issue of any of these "other" sins, they would counsel you to flee fornication, stop stealing, etc. etc. However if you go to them concerning divorcing your spouse, having come to the realization that the decision you made was not the correct decision, accepting that you saw all the signs and naively overlooked them or was simply being stubborn and didn't want to listen, they will not- and possibly cannot, tell you to divorce, end a marriage.

To them, I believe, it doesn't matter whether the marriage began ill-advised and for the wrong reasons or what have you; the fact is, you made a promise, before God and man, to carry out the words that came out of your mouth. Well it's good thing I'm not a preacher or a Christian counselor.

As I write this, I am well aware of the backlash that I am going to receive from those against divorce. Nevertheless, I am compelled to share with you that this section is not pro-divorce, but pro-forgiveness.

Yes, I know that The Word says God never intended for divorce to happen, and that Moses came up with divorce as a solution because of our….hearts. Nevertheless, there are still a few burning questions that come to mind: if God did not want you to marry the person that you are married to… in the first place…, is that marriage considered sinful?

Are you more focused on being a wife/husband than truly pleasing God? Which one is more important when it comes to having and developing your relationship with The Most High? Speaking from experience…if the marriage is NOT what God wanted for your life, you are out of his perfect will. (In my Jersey accent)… "Girl, let me tell you!"

Many of you reading this have heard of God's *perfect* will and God's *permissive* will. And let me reiterate, I am not pro-divorce. I am pro-forgiveness. Having said that, let's move forward with God's perfect and permissive will… according to the doctrine of Brigette.

For those of you that may not have heard these terms, allow me to briefly share with you the story of the births of Ishmael and Isaac. God had spoken to Abraham and Sarah promising that Sarah would bring forth a child. Many, many, many, many, maanny years pass and no baby. So, Sarah, being like so many of us women, gets to thinking that *maybe* God meant that she would give Abraham a son through her maid- Hagar. She, Sarah, approaches her husband Abraham, shares her thoughts, he agrees… (just like a man)… and Hagar gets pregnant and gives birth to Ishmael.

God then tells Abraham that was *not* what He said He would do, nor how He would do it. Nevertheless, God being cool like that, promised Abraham that He would bless Ishmael since he was his son. This was God's <u>permissive</u> will. It wasn't HIS plan, but He can, could, and did deal with it.

The thing about God's *permissive* will is that you may be blessed, as was Ishmael, but you will not receive His **fullness**. The story of Ishmael continues on with him and his mother being exiled from Abraham because of some baby mama foolishness. Ishmael, as a result, had to grow up away from his father and his father's instruction. They did not celebrate his bar mitzvah. He did not get to know his brother or… rub his brothers' back. Abraham didn't get to know his grandbabies… on and on. Although he, Ishmael, was blessed, and he had no control over his birth, he did not receive the same things that Isaac did. I invite you to read his story in the book of Genesis chapter 16.

Isaac, on the other hand, was the promised child. Sarah gave birth to Isaac as God had promised, albeit when she was passed her child bearing years. Consequently, as the promise from God, Isaac was able to take full advantage of being around both his father, Abraham, and his mother. Isaac received life lessons, faith lessons, could watch his father, play with his father, and learn from his father. This is God's perfect will.

While I believe there are blessings in staying married after you become aware that you married under the wrong pretenses, the reality is that unless you *both* come together and *agree* that: 1) a poor decision was made and 2) determine new reasons for remaining together (and staying together "for the kids' sake" is not an acceptable reason because the kids will leave) you will fail.

The Bible, in the book of Amos, asks a very poignant question, "How can two walk together unless they agree?"

Divorce is not easy. In fact, it is very painful...spiritually and emotionally. My experience with divorce went something like this. Once I committed to the divorce from my son's father, God started working on my damaged heart, mind, and emotions. Although I thought I had remained in the relationship because I loved him (the ex-husband), God revealed my true nature. I had harbored hatred deeply in my heart for many years.

One night God woke me up in the middle of the night and had me lay face down on the floor. As I lay prostrate on the floor, God began to expose the truth about what I hid in my heart, mind, and emotions. Slowly I became truthful with myself and with God. I just lay there, with tears flowing from my eyes, saying "Yes, Lord." I don't remember getting up from the floor, but I do know my life changed instantaneously. Doors for better employment opened almost immediately and the rise from this low point began.

You see, when I stood before the preacher that married us, I heard voices screaming "NOOOOOOOOOOO!!!!!!" as the marriage vow questions were asked. In December of 1996, at the age of 25, I was still in bondage to the fear of being abandoned and left alone. My son's father, who was 12 years older than I, had his various issues as well. As a result, neither one of us was equipped to enter into marriage. Neither one of us was emotionally healthy or whole.

I wish I could say that no one told me not to get married, but I cannot. There was one preacher that said, "I don't see anything in your relationship" and therefore he would not advise us to get married...but later said he would do the ceremony for a fee. He did not marry us. But the marriage also ended in August 1999.

Why is it that we, as Christians, try to give sin hierarchy? We shun single mothers, for instance, but embrace fornicating preachers. In some churches, children born "out of wedlock" are not allowed to christened, have a blessing ceremony even though in the story of Ishmael, God personally blessed him.

And when it comes to getting a divorce, we will seek counseling, fast, pray, seminar, separate, and even live apart before we end something that we know deep in our hearts was not of God in the first place. Why do we give sin hierarchy? I guess I will have to chalk this one up to the human condition.

Again, I want to truthfully express that I confer that God never intended for us to divorce, nevertheless divorce does happen and you will be ok. If you have experienced divorce, I challenge you to get some healing. If you are considering divorce, understand that it will be painful, emotionally and spiritually, but there is healing on the other side.

If you decide to remain and uphold the vows that you took, understand that unless you are both willing, nothing is going to change. And even if you are in God's permissive will, it truly is not His best for you. Lastly, and above all else, know that God loves you and will forgive you and cleanse you from all unrighteousness.

CHAPTER 10:

PROPER NUTRITION- LOVE THY SELF

The way you treat yourself sets the standard for others.

~ Sonya Friedman

There are several women whose husbands actively call them all sorts of bitches and not as a derogatory term of endearment either. There are also husbands whose wives actively call them "little boy." I have often wondered why these people stay in these toxic relationships where there is constantly and blatantly no respect.

Yet, when asked these people say "he/she loves and understands me." Why do these people think this is love? Why do these people stay? Why do grown people consistently attempt to make someone like them, love them, respect them, understand them, appreciate them, desire them, support them and their dreams, and on and on? Are they trying to find where they... belong?

Although the problem is multi-faceted, I want to touch on the two things that I personally believe are the roots of them accepting this type of behavior. First, these people truly do not completely love themselves. Loving yourself requires more than simply brushing your teeth, wiping your butt, and washing your hands afterwards.

When you truly love yourself, you refuse to accept sub-standard treatment form others. With a strong positive self-regard, you know what your worth is and you refuse to allow to anyone to treat you or make you feel less than what you deem you are worth.

Think of having a strong positive self-regard as a luxury car. Although luxury cars require gas to run just like a Chevy Nova, a luxury car requires premium gas for *optimal* running and performance. Now if we are not willing to allow someone to fill our car, an object that depreciates as soon as it is driven off the car lot, with a lower grade of gas, why do we allow someone to put low grade experiences in our lives? Why do we allow ourselves, our environments, our homes, and our mental space to be filled with anything less than premium?

If we do not have strong, positive self-regard, we will continuously allow people to be disrespectful towards us. Yes. Yes, I am well aware of derogatory terms being used as terms of endearment, however in the instances I am referring, they are being said in malicious, destructive, and hurtful ways. And that is not acceptable.

If you truly love yourself and have strong positive self-regard, just as I established boundaries for arguing with my husband and assertively stated to him that I would not be spoken to in a condescending manner, you also must establish and operate unyieldingly within those parameters. Love yourself enough to say, this is not ok and I will not accept this type of behavior or treatment directed toward me. I may not be able to stop him/her from doing it, but I can walk away and not allow myself to listen.

Your friends, associates, and your inner circle have a great amount of influence on you. According to researchers at Harvard Medical School, your friends, associates, inner circle play just as much a roll in your successes, self-esteem and obesity as does genetics, family environment and other typical outward things. Fancy that. That's why programs like Weight Watchers are so successful, because they incorporate a buddy system to into their program. Not only are these people likeminded, they are supportive and provide encouragement and positivity.

Secondly, I believe the problem lies with understanding the differences between an expectation and a guarantee as stated earlier in this book. Take the opportunity to review the differences and really ponder what it is you desire to accomplish and gain from your partner, out of your work relationships, from various family members and your siblings. Set the standard and don't allow cheap gas to fill your thoughts.

How to Love You

In life we often get so focused on trying to correct someone else's thinking and behavior when it's us with wrong thinking and behavior. Years ago, a gentleman by the name of Emmanuel Godsson was teaching a lesson on this very topic. In my imagination I see and hear Him lecturing His pupils accordingly:

> "Why are you worried about a speck in your friend's eye when you have a big ass log in your own? How can you even think of saying to your friend, 'Let me help you get rid of that little speck in your eye,' when you can't see past that big ass log in your own eye? Trifling hypocrite! You got life messed up! First, get rid of that log in your own foolish eye; then you will be able to see better and well enough to help deal with the speck in your friend's eye. Just trifling!"

So I embellished Matthew 7: 4-5 a bit. I did say it was my imagination. None-the-less, how often have we all been guilty of such behavior? In our quest to become, sometimes we get so focused on trying to fix someone else and their problems, we don't realize that we are the one standing on the outside, in the pouring rain, dripping wet while they are on the inside dry, warm, and cozy.

All humans, some more than others, have the tendency to clearly see and smell someone else's shit, yet are unable to smell their own. Consider it. We all do it… release excrement.

Recall a time when you've taken a dump, had the doors closed and all. You don't smell your own shit. But if someone is in the house with you, they start yelling, "Ewww! You stink! Spray some air freshener! Did something crawl inside you and die!?" And sometimes even hours have we've released those toxins, the odor still lingers on.

While it is natural to smell someone else's toxins, maturity teaches us that even if we don't smell ourselves, we stink too. We know this because someone else has pointed that out before. Therefore, we need to be mindful of taking care of our hygiene… physical, mental, and spiritual.

Until we learn to love our whole selves, we will remain perpetually torn and continuously walking back across the street to that old signpost, never accomplishing our fullest potential or living the fullest life. You **must** learn to love yourself. And the way you love yourself, is expressed in how you allow others to treat you.

We have to diligently get our house… **self**… in order first, before we can be any good to someone else. We cannot go around trying to help someone else yet we smell of death and destruction. Would you take investment advice from someone with bad credit or parenting advice from a child abuser?

In caring for our mental hygiene, we must learn who "self" is. We must learn to love self... flaws and all. We must learn to express self. Until we can do these three things- know who self is, love self, express self- effectively and efficiently- it is my personal belief that we will be incapable of giving and receiving love, be successful, or live a full life.

People often confuse knowing self, loving self, and expressing self as being selfish. So they go through life not taking the opportunity to know who they are, love who they are, and not express who they are… all because they don't want to be called or be identified as selfish.

But without knowing who you are, how do you determine what you are to become? Without loving who you are, how do you properly love who someone else is? Without expressing who you are, how do you mitigate being mistreated, abused, and misused?

It has been said that we ought to think more highly of others than we do ourselves. This is a principle in humility, of being humble. Yet people tend to misunderstand this principle and, personally, I think it has been misused and incorrectly taught to foster low self-esteem.

Being humble has nothing to do with low self-esteem, being pseudo-modest, or being ostentatious. One definition of humble was "grounded." When I think of the word grounded and things that are grounded, I always think of trees. Their roots hold firm not allowing them to be blown away by every little wind or storm they encounter.

Have you ever really looked at trees? How beautiful and diverse they are. With trunks thick and strong, roots deep and sturdy, their branches reach up high and stretch wide, extending out to provide shelter and shade. To me, trees are nature's example of humbleness. I believe, therefore, that being humble is about having a high, healthy, realistic view of whom you are (being grounded), being able to stretch your "limbs" out to provide shade and shelter, while still being able to rejoice in the uniqueness, beauty, and accomplishments of others.

Anyone who knows me well, will tell you that Brigette loves her some Brigette. I simply love me. Brigette takes care of Brigette. Brigette regularly treats Brigette to ice cream (*That's How I Roll* at Cold Stone Creamery is bomb). Brigette takes Brigette shoe shopping… Brigette has treated herself to The Body Shop ® so often that now her skin rejects lesser quality. Brigette doesn't let anyone piss on her and call her wet…

whatever that means. Brigette loves on Brigette and regularly shows Brigette love and approval for all she is, does, wants to do and desires to become.

Nevertheless, whenever my friends accomplish **_anything_**, ANYTHING... Brigette is their biggest cheerleader! If they are in need, Brigette will give her last and never look for it in return; if they have some crazy far-reaching dream, Brigette sees the vision and co-signs their desires. Why? Just like those trees, Brigette is grounded and can stretch out her limbs to shelter and shade others. She does not suffer from a poor self-image and therefore can appreciate uniqueness, beauty, and the accomplishments of others.

I can see myself playing spades with First Lady Michelle. I see myself being able to sit and have lunch with Ursula and Tyler, talking like we've been friends since 19-whenever. Seriously I do. And I can also sit down in the soup kitchen, next to the smelly, unkempt homeless person and talk about all the conspiracy theories floating around in the world today.

That is humility.

Self and Health

As previously mentioned, your friends, associates, your inner circle have a great amount of influence on you, which is why programs like Weight Watchers is so successful, because they incorporate a buddy system to into their program. Allow me to share my sister's journey to a healthier her.

From as far back as I can remember, my sister has always been plumper than me. Since most of my family members wore double digit clothing, it was just our norm. My grandmother and I were the odd men- or women- out.

It was during a particular period of difficulty in my sister's life, she was looking at some old pictures of herself and she realized that she had been steadily gaining weight. She decided that day that she would do something about it. She wanted change... for herself. After she made that determination things started to change for her.

As the Universe would have it, she enrolled in the local college to complete her degree and had to walk around the campus. Soon another door opened and they would purchase a new home in a beautiful neighborhood with rolling hills. She told me that she bought her some new shoes and started walking around the neighborhood to "...look at all the pretty houses." Truth is she didn't call it exercise.

As she continued to study health and nutrition, she slowly changed the family diet, buying better foods, limiting snacks, baking the chicken, and not eating large quantities of beef. In a few months, a little over a year, my sister went from a size 22 to a size 12! That's 10 dress sizes! It was such a rapid change, rumors started flying... you know how family will do. Today, six years later, my sister maintains her weight, has joined a walking club, and is as beautiful but much healthier because **she** chose to take better care of self and not accept an old family norm.

If you are one of those people that struggle with a low self-image, I encourage you to take charge of that. I write this with the full knowledge that depression is real and sometimes it does require medication. If you feel that it is something chemical that isn't properly balanced, by all means seek professional help.

If you just need someone to talk to and money isn't an issue, seek professional help. If money is an issue, the local library (it's free), Amazon, Half-Priced Books, and others are your best friends with tons of resources. But for the rest of you that are choosing to walk the path I walked, there is much work ahead.

Get in front of that mirror and have that speech!

Tell yourself that you may not be the most beautiful person in the world but you damned sure aren't the ugliest… You are ok. And tell yourself this until you can see that you really are ok… and nothing is wrong with ok. I am reminded of a song by the Nicholas Family entitled *Trees*.

Trees don't want to be mountains, they just praise the Lord. Mountains never are valleys, they just praise the Lord. The sun, the moon, the stars are happy in their heavenly place.
The rivers and the oceans they keep moving from place to place. So if I want to be a servant of The Man who made the trees, I've got to live the life He wants me to live.

Dating Yourself

One of the things that I find that keeps me grounded and centered is taking me out on a date. I purposely spend quality time alone. Being alone gives you the opportunity to search were your attention and loyalties lay. If it's nothing but sitting in my car, I do it. One of my favorite things to do on Sundays is drive around to the "rich people" neighborhoods and I visualize myself having parties and holiday dinners with family and friends.

Sundays are also great because that's when most open houses are held. And although real estate agents hate to see you coming, they can't stop you from looking. Many agents also now have a virtual open house, which I also love. You can check out the web and save the some gas money.

Once I took myself out to dinner and I found out that I don't enjoy eating alone. I guess I feel with dinner should come conversation, so I have never done that again. I will however hang out in the DSW® clearance section for hours on end. But whatever it is you enjoy doing alone, do it and enjoy just being.

Meditation, Reflection, and Thought Discipline

Regardless of your religious or non-religious beliefs, the principles of meditation, reflection and thought discipline can be found in them all. In Christianity, meditation is done to stimulate thought. Taken from the Latin word which means to concentrate, Christian mediation is the process of focusing intently on specific scripture and reflecting on their meaning in the context of the love of God. Psalms 1: 1-2 tells us that a man/woman that doesn't walk in ungodly counsel, stand in sinners' paths, sit with contempt people but finds delight in the law is blessed. Additionally, God charges us to......................
"Be still and know..."

Enough said.

CHAPTER 11:

NOURISHING OTHERS

Greater love hath no man than this: that a man lay down his life for his friends.

~ Jesus

Once you have mastered the skill and art of loving yourself, being able to give love to and receive love from another person becomes possible. The experiences of the many individuals I spoke with while doing research for this book is a testament to that fact. It was only after each individual learned to truly love themselves by:

1) accepting their imperfections,
2) accepting their quirks,
3) accepting their past failures and
4) fully understood that they are human and subjected to occasionally failing,

did real love walk, seemingly, into their lives.

Once you've come into the full knowledge of *you* and all of your flaws, you become less likely to impose standards of perfection on another human being. You readily understand the failings and misfortunes of others because you know first-hand how diligently you've tried to be perfect... and how miserably you have failed. This understanding, this knowledge and acceptance of your whole self, can be summed up in one word. What you have accomplished and earned is the skillful art of... forgiveness.

Because you have developed the ability to forgive yourself, you can now begin to forgive the misgivings and shortcomings of others. There are hundreds of best-selling books about forgiveness so I won't belabor how important it is. I will say, however, that forgiveness really is a simple thing.

The root all lies in understanding that YOU are not perfect, and until you *are* perfect, YOU cannot and should not expect perfection from anyone else. Therefore, YOU should forgive. If you want your misdeeds (or *Mr. Deeds*... Hey Tyler!!! Hey!!!) pardoned, you must... must pardon the misdeeds of others. It's that simple.

You cannot love... I repeat... you CANNOT love, without knowing how to forgive. This is why God is Love... He knows how to forgive!

Jesus, on the cross, after being whipped and beaten, tortured, teased, and tormented as He hung there between two trifling ass mu.... (clears throat... you know what I'm saying...) showed the ultimate example of true love. "Father, Forgive them..."

Mercy!! MERCY!!

The Lord knew that could *not* have been meeee up there on that cross! That pain would have gotten to a sistah and I would have called all the angels down from heaven, all the demons up from hell, the Army, Navy, Air Force, and the Marines! and had them all wreaking havoc on top of Calvary, throughout Jerusalem, Damascus, Judea, Samaria, and Capernaum! HA! I ain't lying, y'all! I ain't lying!!! Y'all better be glad my name is Brigette and not Yeshua!... Whew!

But, I've digressed (flips hair, pats forehead).

Forgiveness the Prerequisite for Loving Others

At some point in your life you have undoubtedly heard someone say, "Forgive and you will be forgiven." So opposing reason would indicate that if one doesn't forgive, you would also *not* be forgiven. This is as simple as eating ice cream.

Additionally, it reminds me of the agriculture and the water in the glass discussion... What you plant, you pick. What you pour *in* the glass is what you pour *out* the glass.

Forgive. Get forgiven.

It doesn't matter if your brother-in-law molested your daughters. Forgive him. You don't have to like him, invite him to your home for the holidays, or attend his funeral. Forgive him.

It doesn't matter if your mama ruined your credit score before you could even spell *cred* or *it*... forgive her. You don't have to let her "hold your card" and you don't have to fund her bingo habit. Forgive her.

It doesn't matter if your wife took your son, all the furniture and nice cookware, and left you with an empty home, a bed you didn't want in the first place, and her wedding dress. Forgive her. Keep doing your duties as your child's father; don't make other females pay for her vindictive behavior. Forgive her.

It doesn't matter if your mother told you she was going to the store and didn't promptly return; it doesn't matter that when she finally returned from the store you were grown; it doesn't matter that a small community of people failed to recognize you and your siblings as the children of your deceased parent; it doesn't matter if that deceased parent threw away the first book you wrote and it took you twenty-three years, three children, two divorces, being fired from your last two full-time jobs, being evicted, and being homeless to open up the laptop and complete a book that you thought of a good title for book in the spring of 2004, while riding around late at night in Round Rock, Texas, coming from getting a What-A-Burger with cheese, no onion, onion rings instead of fries and a strawberry shake, with your dear friend whom you initially tried to hook up with your present husband! Forgive! And let love walk in.

The Power of Forgiveness

When I think of the power of forgiveness, my mind goes deep into the soil with a geminating seed. Germination is the process when the plant *breaks forth* and beings to *emerge,* to surface, to rise about from the soil. I must admit that this also reminds me of the child birthing process.

The seed, therefore, has completed two key changes: it has taken root *and* it has given birth. It has pushed <u>down</u>, for stability and strength, as it has push <u>out</u> for expansion into something greater than its beginnings! It has pushed, at the same time... both **down** and **out**. The thought of that simply amazes me, yet every woman that has given birth vaginally knows exactly how you can simultaneously push down and out... bringing forth new life.

When you forgive, the core that keeps you stable takes a stronghold, causing you to become unwavering, firm, and strong enough to withstand all the tsunamis and tornadoes life throws your way. You will be able to be steadfast, unmovable, always abounding, plentiful, multiplying, adding, increasing, and producing! How else do you think Oprah has amassed all of the things she has? Yes, she worked hard. Yes, she prepared. Yes, she planned. But before she really began to truly grow, she... forgave.

When you forgive, the plant that springs from those dirty places, those places of bitterness, of pulling on locked doors, of controlling behaviors, of all those places that once held you below the surface of your destiny, now becomes stronger and stronger, healthier and healthier. By continually forgiving and letting go of old shit, that new plant will bring forth shade for your comfort and protection from the sun, and will eventually begin to bring forth fruit... food... sustenance... love.

And as one tree- ONE- bears multiply fruit, that individual tree is able to feed, to nourish... to express love towards... multiply people. With a continuous regime of proper care; with continued pruning, feeding, watering, nurturing, that ONE tree will continue to provide loving nourishment to others.

If one tree can do all of this, imagine what two trees that have let go, broke forth, and have begun to produce fruit can do.

Imagine what twenty trees could do. Fifty trees. A community of trees. A world of trees.

I will close this chapter with a question a woman posted in a Facebook forum. The answer to her question is what this chapter is all about... why this book is ultimately written. As you read it, see if you can relate to her struggle and if you can identify many of the things we have already discussed throughout this book. When you are done, send a vesper her way:

"When we got married 4 yrs. ago, my husband was trying to finish law school. I worked two jobs to support us until he finished, studied and passed the bar exam. The deal was after that, he would work and I would focus on finishing my Master's degree. Well, he graduated and all that started a great job last year. Now he has decided we have grown apart, he is no longer in love w/ me and he wants a divorce. I got a lawyer and I'm determined to take his azz to the cleaners on this. I sacrificed, worked two jobs and he decides he wants to bail on our marriage??? Hell no. My parents said to stop fighting him about money, and start moving on. I can't do it. He OWES me. What do you think?" ....

Let that sh*t go!

AN EMOTIONAL ENEMA

It releases and relieves.

It flushes away.

It cleanses and disinfects.

It humbles.

It makes whole.

Forgiveness… is… powerful.

Forgiveness is…

An Emotional Enema.

You are now un-constipated. You are now ready to love.

FINAL THOUGHTS...

FINAL THOUGHTS

The hardest thing to do is transition. Having grown up in a very affluent family and household, and not knowing what it meant to be without or not have as a child, transitioning and experiencing lack as an adult was not easy for me. But I made it.

I did not intend for this book to be "churchy" but, as I've stated in previous chapters, what is in you will come out. My beliefs are a major part of who I am. This is not to say that there are no other paths to get to the same goal of physical, emotional, and spiritual heath. The world is too big for that. If the Universe meant for all of us to travel the same path, I'm sure it would be only one path. Yet, many paths lead to the same destination. Even if there is only One bridge.

Whatever method you choose in achieving emotional health does not matter to me… as long as you choose one. Get healthy emotionally.
Love yourself.
Love on yourself.
Be happy. Be healed. Be whole.
Let all of that old, compacted, thick, pore clogging, body disfiguring, mind altering shit GO! LET IT GO!

The change you seek may not come the way you feel it should or think it can, but change will come. Even if that means, the change is in you. .